Spinoza

Classic Thinkers

Richard T. W. Arthur, *Leibniz*
Terrell Carver, *Marx*
Daniel E. Flage, *Berkeley*
J. M. Fritzman, *Hegel*
Bernard Gert, *Hobbes*
Thomas Kemple, *Simmel*
Ralph McInerny, *Aquinas*
Dale E. Miller, *J. S. Mill*
Joanne Paul, *Thomas More*
William J. Prior, *Socrates*
A. J. Pyle, *Locke*
James T. Schleifer, *Tocqueville*
Céline Spector, *Rousseau*
Andrew Ward, *Kant*

Spinoza

Justin Steinberg and Valtteri Viljanen

polity

First published in 2021 by Polity Press

Polity Press
65 Bridge Street
Cambridge CB2 1UR, UK

Polity Press
101 Station Landing
Suite 300
Medford, MA 02155, USA

ISBN-13: 978-0-7456-6489-7
ISBN-13: 978-0-7456-6490-3(pb)

A catalogue record for this book is available from the British Library.

Library of Congress Cataloging-in-Publication Data

Names: Steinberg, Justin (Associate Professor of Philosophy), author. | Viljanen, Valtteri, author.
Title: Spinoza / Justin Steinberg and Valtteri Viljanen.
Description: Cambridge, UK ; Medford, MA, USA : Polity Press, 2020. | Series: Classic thinkers | Includes bibliographical references and index. | Summary: "The definitive guide to the fascinating and controversial thought of one of history's most important philosophers"-- Provided by publisher.
Identifiers: LCCN 2020014307 (print) | LCCN 2020014308 (ebook) | ISBN 9780745664897 (hardback) | ISBN 9780745664903 (paperback) | ISBN 9781509544967 (epub)
Subjects: LCSH: Spinoza, Benedictus de, 1632-1677.
Classification: LCC B3998 .S78648 2020 (print) | LCC B3998 (ebook) | DDC 199/.492--dc23
LC record available at https://lccn.loc.gov/2020014307
LC ebook record available at https://lccn.loc.gov/2020014308

Typeset in 10.5 on 12pt Palatino
by Fakenham Prepress Solutions, Fakenham, Norfolk NR21 8NL
Printed and bound in Great Britain by CPI Group (UK) Ltd, Croydon

For further information on Polity, visit our website: politybooks.com

Contents

Detailed Contents

Primary Sources and Abbreviations

Spinoza's works

All Latin passages refer to (abbreviated as G): *Spinoza Opera* I–IV, ed. Carl Gebhardt. Heidelberg: Carl Winter, 1925.

English translations refer to: *The Collected Works of Spinoza* I–II, trans. and ed. Edwin Curley. Princeton, NJ: Princeton University Press, 1985 and 2016.

Unless otherwise indicated, a reference to a work by Spinoza is to the *Ethics*. References to it open with numerals, which indicate the part, followed by specifying information based on the following abbreviations:

a	axiom
app	appendix
c	corollary
d	demonstration
def	definition
defaff	definition of the affects (in the third part of the *Ethics*)
exp	explanation
le	lemma
po	postulate
pref	preface
s	scholium

For instance, 1p8s2 refers to the second scholium of the eighth proposition in the first part of the *Ethics*.

References to the *Tractatus Theologico-Politicus* open with an abbreviated reference to the work – TTP – followed by the chapter and section in the Curley translation and often by a reference to the Gebhardt volume and page. For instance, TTP 3.28; G III, 50 refers to chapter 3, section 28; Gebhardt volume 3, page 50.

References to the *Tractatus Politicus* open with an abbreviated reference to the work – TP – followed by the chapter and section. For instance, TP 4/1 refers to chapter 4, section 1.

Other works by Spinoza

CM   *Metaphysical Thoughts (Cogitata Metaphysica)*
Ep.   *Correspondence (Epistolae)*
KV   *Short Treatise on God, Man and His Well-being (Korte Verhandeling van God, de Mensch, en des zelfs Welstand)*
NS   *De nagelate schriften*
TIE   *Treatise on the Emendation of the Intellect (Tractatus de Intellectus Emendatione)*

Other abbreviated references

CSM   René Descartes, *The Philosophical Writings of Descartes* I–II, trans. John Cottingham, Robert Stoothoff, and Dugald Murdoch. Cambridge: Cambridge University Press, 1985.
CSMK   René Descartes, *The Philosophical Writings of Descartes III: The Correspondence*, trans. John Cottingham, Robert Stoothoff, Dugald Murdoch, and Anthony Kenny. Cambridge: Cambridge University Press, 1991.
CWA   Aristotle. *The Complete Works of Aristotle: The Revised Oxford Translation* I–II, ed. Jonathan Barnes. Princeton, NJ: Princeton University Press, 1984.
EW   Thomas Hobbes, *The English Works of Thomas Hobbes* I–XI, ed. William Molesworth. London: John Bohn, 1839–1845.

Acknowledgments

We would like to begin by warmly thanking the people at Polity – Ellen MacDonald-Kramer, Evie Deavall, Pascal Porcheron, and Gail Ferguson – for their patience, expertise, and effort in bringing the process to completion. We are also very grateful to the two anonymous reviewers for their extremely helpful reports.

This monograph contains, in an adapted form and as indicated in the notes, material from the following original publications:

Justin Steinberg, 2018. *Spinoza's Political Psychology: The Taming of Fortune and Fear.* Cambridge: Cambridge University Press.

Valtteri Viljanen, 2009. "Spinoza's Ontology," in Olli Koistinen (ed.), *The Cambridge Companion to Spinoza's* Ethics, pp. 56–78. Cambridge: Cambridge University Press.

Valtteri Viljanen, 2015. "Theory of *Conatus,*" in André Santos Campos (ed.), *Spinoza: Basic Concepts,* pp. 95–105. Exeter: Imprint Academic.

Permission to incorporate this material into the present work is gratefully acknowledged.

Finally, we would like to acknowledge that the work on this monograph has been financially supported by the Academy of Finland (project number 275583).

1

Spinoza's Life

1.1 Early life in Amsterdam[1]

Baruch Spinoza was born in Amsterdam on November 24, 1632. He came from a family of Portuguese *converso* Jews, or Jews who were forced to convert outwardly to Christianity after Judaism was prohibited in Spain and Portugal in the fifteenth century. His father's family emigrated to the Netherlands near the turn of the seventeenth century, when the Netherlands were fighting for independence from the Spanish Hapsburgs in the so-called Dutch Revolt (1568–1648). The aspiring republic cautiously admitted Jews, recognizing that many of these *conversos* were experienced merchants who maintained trade connections with Portugal and its colonies. In addition to the economic reasons for allowing Jewish settlement, there were also theological and ideological motivations: Dutch Calvinists conceived of themselves as the New Israelites, identifying to some degree with the plight of the Jews; and, more pragmatically, they hoped that the Jews might help to teach them Hebrew so that they could read the Hebrew Bible directly. Still, Jews were regarded with mistrust and were accorded a rather precarious status in Dutch society. Their teachings were monitored for blasphemy, and they were not formally admitted as Dutch subjects until 1657.

The Amsterdam Jewish community in which Spinoza was raised was small and tight-knit, comprised of roughly two thousand members in the middle of the seventeenth century. They occupied a vibrant, bustling neighborhood of Vlooienburg (also known as

Jodenbuurt), which was home not only to Jews but also to some Christians, including the renowned painter Rembrandt van Rijn, who lived in the Jewish Quarter between 1639 and 1658, very near Spinoza's family home. Spinoza's father Michael was a respected and relatively successful member of this community. He was a merchant who imported dried fruit, among other things. And he served for some time on the *parnassim*, a board of elders who governed the affairs of the Jewish community and who served as liaisons to the Dutch authorities.

While we know disappointingly little about the early years of Spinoza's life, we do know that he – who at the time was known as Bento and Baruch, meaning "blessed [one]" in Portuguese and Hebrew, respectively – started his studies at a rather young age in the well-regarded Talmud Torah school. Here he would have studied Hebrew, the 24 books in the Hebrew Bible, and parts of Jewish law derived from the Oral Torah, or Talmud. One of the most prominent teachers at the school was Menasseh ben Israel, a rabbi who engaged with unorthodox thought, such as the work of the French Calvinist theologian Isaac La Peyrère. But the rabbi who is more likely to have been a proper teacher to Spinoza was Saul Levi Morteira, a respected Talmudist, whose weekly study group Spinoza would attend even after he had to abandon his formal schooling at the age of 14 to work in his father's business. Through Morteira, Spinoza was likely introduced to the works of rationalist Jewish philosophers like Saadia Gaon, Gersonides, and, most importantly, Maimonides.

Some time in his early twenties (in the mid-1650s), Spinoza sought to learn Latin, the language of philosophy and natural science. This led him to another formative intellectual influence in his life: his Latin teacher, Franciscus van den Enden (1602–1674). Van den Enden is a very interesting figure in his own right. He was an apostate Jesuit (and a suspected atheist), a medical doctor, a radical egalitarian, and an abolitionist with a fierce anticlerical streak. He was put to death in 1674, having been found guilty of conspiring to depose the king of France, Louis XIV, in order to establish a free republic in Normandy. And his political ideas, expressed for instance in his *Free Political Propositions and Considerations of the State* (1665), might well have influenced Spinoza's own political thought.[2] The lessons at Van den Enden's school would have opened up new horizons of thought for the young Spinoza, who would come to be known by the Latinized version of his name: Benedictus or Benedict. They read classical history, literature, and philosophy from such authors as Seneca, Horace, Tacitus, Ovid, Livy, and Cicero. The school also put on productions of Terence's plays in which it is thought that Spinoza participated. It is also likely that Van den Enden would have introduced Spinoza to the "new science" of Bacon, Galileo, and Descartes, as well as to the bold political theories of Machiavelli and Hobbes. These ideas, together with the Jewish thought of his earlier education, provided a foundation and orientation for the development of Spinoza's original philosophical system. Through his involvement in Van den Enden's school, Spinoza would also have gotten to know many members of a group of Collegiants, heterodoxical religious thinkers (including Lutherans, Mennonites, Quakers, Arminians, and Anabaptists) who formed what they called "colleges" that met every other Sunday. Several of these Collegiants would later become part of Spinoza's philosophical circle, including Simon de Vries, Pieter Balling, Jarig Jellesz, and his future publisher Jan Rieuwertsz.

Spinoza's involvement with this group of freethinkers would have given him a foothold on intellectual life outside of the Jewish community. In the meantime, during this period, he witnessed and grieved the deaths of one family member after another, resulting in a further loosening of his connection to the Jewish community. His birth mother, Hanna, had died when he was just six in 1638; his brother Isaac died in 1649; and in a span of three years (1651–1654) his sister Miriam, his stepmother Esther, who helped to raise him, and his father all died. Spinoza would write in the *Ethics* that "[a] free man thinks of nothing less than of death, and his wisdom is a meditation on life, not on death" (4p67), but it is hard to imagine Spinoza at this stage in his life maintaining the high-minded perspective of a free person. At any rate, the death of his father in 1654, when Spinoza was just 21, left him and his younger brother Gabriel to run the family business.

His life as head of a business did not last long. On July 27, 1656, a *cherem* – a complete excommunication from the Jewish congregation and community – was pronounced against Spinoza. The insecure social position of Amsterdam Jews encouraged elders to wield the punishment of *cherem* as a form of communal protection so as not to fall afoul of Dutch mores. The importance of enforcing standards of religious propriety was perhaps heightened at this moment, as Rabbi ben Israel was negotiating with Oliver Cromwell for the readmission of Jews into England, and as Jews were finally on the cusp of achieving full recognition as subjects of the Dutch Republic.

Spinoza was hardly the first member of the community to receive this treatment. Ironically, ben Israel himself had been banned – though only for a single day – for a minor form of malfeasance. A more disturbing precedent was the *cherem* of Uriel da Costa, who in 1640 (when Spinoza was just eight years old) was cast out of the community for denying the immortality of the soul and challenging the status of the Torah as divine revelation. A *cherem* was typically followed by an invitation to renounce one's offensive beliefs and rejoin the community, and, in da Costa's case, the condition of readmission was that he was publicly whipped and forced to lie down just outside of the synagogue, where he was ignominiously trampled by congregants. Just days after being subjected to these humiliations, he took his own life.

Spinoza's *cherem* was distinctive in its severity, and he was cast out permanently and unconditionally. The text of the pronouncement reads:

> The Lords of the *ma'amad*, having long known of the evil opinions and acts of Baruch de Spinoza, have endeavored by various means and promises, to turn him from his evil ways. But having failed to make him mend his wicked ways, and, on the contrary, daily receiving more and more serious information about the abominable heresies which he practiced and taught and about his monstrous deeds, and having for this numerous trustworthy witnesses who have deposed and born witness to this effect in the presence of the said Espinoza, they became convinced of the truth of this matter; and after all of this has been investigated in the presence of the honorable *chachamim*, they have decided, with their consent, that the said Espinoza should be excommunicated and expelled from the people of Israel. By decree of the angels and by the command of the holy men, we excommunicate, expel, curse and damn Baruch de Espinoza, with the consent of God, Blessed be He, and with the consent of the entire holy congregation, and in front of these holy scrolls with the 613 precepts which are written therein; cursing him with the excommunication with which Joshua banned Jericho and with the curse which Elisha cursed the boys and with all the castigations that are written in the Book of the Law. Cursed be he by day and cursed be he by night; cursed be he when he lies down and cursed be he when he rises up. Cursed be he when he goes out and cursed be he when he comes in. The Lord will not spare him, but then the anger of the Lord and his jealousy shall smoke against that man, and all the curses that are written in this book shall lie upon him, and the Lord shall blot out his name from under heaven. And the Lord shall separate him unto evil out of all the tribes of Israel, according to all the curses of the covenant that

are written in this book of the law. But you that cleave unto the Lord your God are alive every one of you this day.

While the nature of the "abominable heresies" and "monstrous deeds" that Spinoza is accused of committing remains something of a mystery, it is likely that he was censured for, among other things, denying the existence of a personal, caring God, denying that Scripture was divinely revealed, and denying that there is a separable soul that could survive physical death.

Even though Spinoza had begun to form ties with Dutch freethinkers, such a decisive expulsion would have carried enormous social costs for anyone. Spinoza was thoroughly cut off from what remained of his family and the rather insular Jewish community of his youth; and he was left to find a new form of employment without the benefit of his communal network in a society that was still deeply suspicious of, if not hostile towards, Jews. And yet, were it not for this experience, it is very unlikely that any of us would know of Spinoza today. From this expulsion, a philosopher was born.

1.2 The young philosopher: after the *cherem*

There is almost no record of what Spinoza's life in Amsterdam was like in the years immediately following the *cherem*. All indications, though, are that Spinoza was remarkably resilient. He probably immersed himself further in Van den Enden's school, likely even lodging there. He also occasionally went to lectures at the University of Leiden, which was at the time a hotbed of Cartesian thought. Notable Cartesian professors there were Adriaan Heereboord, a philosopher of logic, and Johannes de Raey, a former pupil of the great Dutch proponent of Cartesianism, Henricus Regius. Other philosophy students in Leiden at that time who would go on to become friends of Spinoza were Adriaan Koerbagh and Lodewijk Meyer. In the summer of 1661, Spinoza moved to Rijnsburg, a small village near Leiden, maybe to establish closer contact with Leiden Collegiants or perhaps simply to escape some of the distractions of Amsterdam.

Between the *cherem* and the move to Rijnsburg, Spinoza began composing what is likely his first extant manuscript, the unfinished work on method, the *Treatise on the Emendation of the Intellect*. It opens with an inspiring, if rather stylized, autobiographical sketch:

> After experience had taught me that all the things which regularly occur in ordinary life are empty and futile, and I saw that all the things which were the cause or object of my fear had nothing of good or bad in themselves, except insofar as [my] mind was moved by them, I resolved at last to try to figure out whether there was anything which would be the true good, capable of communicating itself, and which alone would affect the mind, all others being rejected – whether there was something which, once found and acquired, would continuously give me the greatest joy, to eternity. (TIE, §1)[3]

He proceeds to clarify that since the chief ends which people pursue – honor, wealth, and sensual pleasure – do not supply lasting satisfaction, he sought to turn his mind away from these things and direct it instead to the "knowledge of the union that the mind has with the whole of Nature" (TIE, §13). If these remarks seem rather out of place in a work on epistemology and method, we must bear in mind that many works of logic or method in this period explicitly aimed at purifying the mind so that one can better know and love God. In any case, the view that philosophy aims to reorient the mind, or heal the intellect, persisted throughout Spinoza's life, underwriting his masterwork, the *Ethics.*

Other elements of this early work prefigure Spinoza's mature philosophy. For instance, he distinguishes the unreliable, if useful, forms of cognition that arise from testimony, language, and "random experience" from the secure knowledge of a thing's essence (TIE, §19). He would refine this epistemic hierarchy throughout his life. He also argues here that true ideas possess the highest certainty (i.e., are self-evident) and so do not depend on extrinsic validation, a point that he also reprised in later writings. But the fact that Spinoza never completed the work suggests that he either remained unsatisfied with certain aspects of it or simply felt that the core ideas were successfully incorporated into later works.

In the early 1660s, Spinoza was also hard at work on two other manuscripts. One was a kind of early, non-geometrical attempt to work out some of the ideas that would be expressed in refined, geometrical form in the *Ethics*. This work, the *Short Treatise on God, Man, and His Well-Being*, begins, like the *Ethics*, with a discussion of God, God's nature as a substance of which all attributes are predicated, and of the properties that follow from this nature, before turning to an account of human nature, human knowledge, the passions, and human blessedness. By providing a window into the full range of Spinoza's early ideas, this text sheds light on Spinoza's development as a philosopher. However, it was never prepared for publication and the extant versions – discovered only in the 1850s – might not be the most reliable expressions of Spinoza's thought since we only have later Dutch copies, while the original work was likely written in Latin and translated into Dutch (perhaps originally by Spinoza himself).

The other work from the period was the only book that was published in Spinoza's name in his lifetime: *Descartes's "Principles of Philosophy"*. As the title would suggest, this is an exposition of, and commentary on, Descartes's textbook (especially *Principles* parts 2 and 3), to which Spinoza appended further ruminations on God, necessity, truth, and many other central preoccupations under the title *Metaphysical Thoughts*. The work – which was written for a student at Leiden University named Johannes Casear (or Casearius), whom Spinoza was tutoring – reconstructs the main claims of Cartesian science in geometrical order. In his introduction to the work, Spinoza's friend Lodewijk Meyer defends the structure of the text on the grounds that the "noble discipline of mathematics" provides the firmest foundations for grounding "the whole edifice of human knowledge" (G I, 127). While Spinoza sought in this work "not to depart a hair's breadth from Descartes' opinion" (G I, 131), Meyer reveals some of the ways in which Spinoza's own thinking was already sharply at odds with Descartes's, including the fact that Spinoza denied both that the human mind is a thinking substance and that we have a free will that is distinct from the intellect. Spinoza's relationship to Cartesianism remained fraught throughout his life. There can be no doubt that Spinoza adopts a fundamentally Cartesian conceptual framework, and Descartes's influence on Spinoza's own intellectual circle can hardly be overstated. Nevertheless, it is equally clear that Spinoza was deeply critical of his revered predecessor, often undermining Descartes's views from within this shared framework. And later in his life, Spinoza would rail against the "stupid Cartesians" who sought to distance themselves from him by publicly denouncing his philosophy (Ep. 68).

While in Rijnsburg, Spinoza took lodging with Herman Homan. In order to earn his living, Spinoza did more than just tutor; he ground lenses for various optical instruments, including microscopes and telescopes. Homan's house, now known as the *Spinozahuis*, can be visited today, and in it one will find a lathe that is much like the one that Spinoza would have used to grind lenses, along with a reconstruction of his personal library at the time of his death. Lens grinding required at once a theoretical grasp of optics and a crafts-person's precision, and Spinoza was evidently quite skilled, as his lenses were sought after, and lauded, by eminent scientists like Christiaan Huygens (1629–1695).

His connection to the larger scientific community would also be aided by his friendship with the theologian, diplomat, and scientist Henry Oldenburg (1620–1677), who was elected as the first secretary of the recently founded Royal Society. From his position at the center of English scientific activity, Oldenburg sent Spinoza work from the groundbreaking chemist and physicist Robert Boyle (1627–1691), to which Spinoza replied in a lengthy letter (Ep. 6). The early exchange with Oldenburg – with whom he would correspond periodically throughout his life – along with his continued application of optical theory, reveals his engagement with the experimental sciences. Still, the picture of Spinoza relayed by his early biographer, Johannes Colerus, captures Spinoza's rationalist, or anti-experimental, cast of mind well: "He also often took his magnifying glass, observing through this the smallest mosquitoes and flies, at the same time reasoning about them. He knows, however, that things cannot be seen as they are in themselves. The eternal properties and laws of things and processes can only be discovered by deduction from common notions and evident axioms."[4]

1.3 The mature Spinoza: Voorburg and The Hague

In 1663, Spinoza moved into the house of Collegiant painter Daniel Tydeman in Voorburg, a village near The Hague. While continuing to ply his trade as a lens grinder, he also kept working towards a comprehensive, precise, and systematized account of his philosophy. By 1665, he seems to have composed a rough draft of the *Ethics*, which at the time was comprised of just three parts that would later be expanded into five. And while he had not yet published anything that would fully reveal his boldness as a thinker, he was gaining a notorious reputation in the general Dutch public as an antireligious thinker. In order to rebut these personal charges and defend the freedom to philosophize in the face of an intolerant Calvinist clergy, Spinoza began work on what would become the *Tractatus Theologico-Politicus* (TTP), or *Theological-Political Treatise*, a daring work of scriptural interpretation and political philosophy.

The TTP was probably long in gestation, perhaps originating in the apology or defense that he allegedly wrote in response to the *cherem*. In a 1665 letter to Oldenburg, he states three reasons for composing the work: to oppose the prejudices of theologians; to rebut the charge of atheism; and to defend the freedom of philosophizing (Ep. 30). Between the time when he first started the work and the time of its eventual publication in 1670, the situation only seemed to get worse for freethinkers in the Netherlands; and in 1668, Spinoza's friend Adriaan Koerbagh was arrested on charges of blasphemy. Koerbagh's imprisonment and subsequent death likely spurred Spinoza to publish the work.

The TTP is a challenging and multifaceted work. In it, Spinoza joins his knowledge of Scripture, dating back to his years at Talmud Torah, to his metaphysical commitments, and caps it all off with an original account of the rights and principles of state governance. The central claim of the text is that Scripture is not a work of metaphysics but rather a book of simple moral teachings. Consequently, we should not regard philosophical arguments about God and God's nature as in conflict with Scripture itself. It also advances further arguments for diminishing clerical authority and for permitting freedom of conscience and expression.

While the TTP was published anonymously and with a false imprint, the identity of the author was soon discovered, and the work was denounced as godless and dangerous. His one-time correspondent Willem van Blijenbergh called it "a book full of studious abominations and an accumulation of opinions which have been forged in hell." Numerous other refutations of the work by prominent authors appeared soon after its publication, with critical responses being written even by some of the same liberal theologians whom Spinoza had hoped to win over. Even Thomas Hobbes, no stranger to controversy, is reported as having remarked upon reading the TTP that the work "cut through him a bar's length, for he durst not write so boldly."[5] It was a mark of Spinoza's well-known caution (he famously wore a ring with the motto "*Caute*," Latin for "caution," on it) that he published the work only in Latin, the language of the educated, personally intervening before a Dutch translation was prepared.

Around the time of the publication of the TTP, Spinoza moved from Voorburg to The Hague. At this point, he likely resumed work on the *Ethics*, maintaining a relatively low profile. However, his attention turned once again to politics in 1672 when King Louis XIV led French troops to invade the United Provinces, capturing a number of Dutch cities. Johan de Witt, who, as Grand Pensionary, occupied the highest political post at the time, was held responsible for not preventing the incursion. And after resigning from the position, he and his brother were viciously killed by a mob. This incident clearly upset the otherwise unflappable Spinoza, who reportedly had to be restrained from confronting the mob.

De Witt was a champion of liberty, and his death marked the end of the purely republican period in the United Provinces where there was no stadtholder or quasi-monarchical figure. Spinoza was both a committed republican and a supporter of the De Witt regime, and it is thought that this episode might have prompted him to begin composing a second work of politics, the *Tractatus Politicus* or *Political Treatise*. This work, which bears the unmistakable influence of Niccolò Machiavelli (1469–1527), explores how political institutions are to be designed so as to promote peace and avoid regime collapses like De Witt's. Unfortunately, it remained unfinished at the time of Spinoza's death, just as he had begun describing the organization of a model democracy. Perhaps more regrettable is that in the few paragraphs that he did write he excluded women from participation in this democracy.

Spinoza was hardly a hermit as he maintained a circle of friends and was apparently quite companionable in general. Still, he valued his privacy. All of that might have changed in 1673, when he was invited by Karl Ludwig, the Elector of Palatine – who evidently had *not* read the TTP – to take up a professorship at the University of Heidelberg. Spinoza declined the invitation, worrying that teaching would limit his own intellectual advancement and that the freedom to philosophize would not be extensive enough to protect him from charges of blasphemy (Ep. 48). Spinoza's caution probably served him well in this instance.

He also seems to have exercised discretion by not publishing the *Ethics* when it was completed in 1675. And he was careful about whom he allowed to read the manuscript. One of the few trusted readers was Ehrenfried Walter von Tschirnhaus (1651–1708), whose correspondence with Spinoza is one of the richest and most illuminating. Almost ten years after Spinoza's death, Tschirnhaus published *The Medicine of the Mind*, a philosophical treatise that clearly bears Spinoza's influence. Tschirnhaus was a friend of the great philosopher Gottfried Wilhelm Leibniz (1646–1716), who was deeply curious about Spinoza's philosophy. While Spinoza directed Tschirnhaus not to let Leibniz read his copy of the *Ethics*, it seems likely that Tschirnhaus did not honor Spinoza's wish, and in 1676 the inquisitive Leibniz travelled to visit and converse with Spinoza. Not much evidence of their legendary meetings survives, but it seems that the two discussed at least Cartesian physics, principles of metaphysics, and the ontological proof of God's existence.

Around the time of Leibniz's visit, Spinoza's health was deteriorating. He had been suffering from a chronic lung condition for many years, exacerbated by the prolonged inhalation of the glass particulates from lens grinding. He died in February 1677 in The Hague. Spinoza's burial four days later gathered a notable crowd of friends and admirers. Soon after his death, his friend and publisher Jan Rieuwertsz printed copies of Spinoza's *Opera Posthuma*, which contained Spinoza's previously unpublished texts, including the TIE, the TP, a work on Hebrew grammar, and his magnum opus, the *Ethics*. While his life was short, he apparently lived well, at least according to the standards of his own philosophy. All reports suggest that he eschewed riches and honors, was generous and kind to those around him, maintained remarkable control of his emotions, and, of course, dedicated himself thoroughly to the pursuit of knowledge. Bertrand Russell's assessment of Spinoza as "the noblest and most lovable of the great philosophers" seems fitting.[6] But, of course, to really understand this lovable philosopher, we must turn directly to his ideas. So let us begin our examination of Spinoza's philosophy.

Further reading

Klever, W. N. A. 1996. "Spinoza's Life and Works," in Don Garrett (ed.), *The Cambridge Companion to Spinoza*, pp. 13–60. Cambridge: Cambridge University Press.

Nadler, Steven. 2018 (1999). *Spinoza: A Life*, 2nd edn. Cambridge: Cambridge University Press.

Steenbakkers, Piet. 2009. "The Textual History of Spinoza's *Ethics*," in Olli Koistinen (ed.), *The Cambridge Companion to Spinoza's Ethics*, pp. 26–41. Cambridge: Cambridge University Press.

Yovel, Yirmiyahu. 1989. *Spinoza and Other Heretics* I. Princeton: Princeton University Press.

2

Reality as God or Nature

Spinoza is famous – or notorious – for his contentious and bold claims concerning the basic nature of reality. This chapter discusses Spinoza's ontology and explains its most salient and direct implications.[1] The three major topics are (1) the basic building blocks of reality, (2) monism, according to which there is only one thing, which is absolutely infinite, and (3) necessitarianism, according to which all things exist and act in the only possible way.[2]

2.1 Substance and mode

In the opening passages of the *Ethics*, Spinoza defines three kinds of basic entities, *substance*, *mode*, and *attribute*, which serve as the bedrock of his metaphysical system. We aim to show that despite his somewhat peculiar vocabulary, there is much in his explication of these concepts that is actually rather traditional and intelligible, as his understanding of these matters harks back to the traditional distinction of substance and accident, or thing and property.

Right at the beginning of the *Ethics*, Spinoza states his definitions of substance and mode:

> By substance I understand what is in itself and is conceived through itself, i.e., that whose concept does not require the concept of another thing, from which it must be formed. (1def3)

> By mode I understand the affections of a substance, *or* that which is in another through which it is also conceived. (1def5)

That substances are in and conceived through themselves, whereas modes are in and conceived through another, clearly implies that substances hold some kind of ontological and epistemological priority over modes. But what kind of priority? For someone proceeding "in geometric order," it is of course of the utmost importance that the starting point of the exposition – definitions and axioms – are clearly stated and cogent. Despite Spinoza's best efforts, however, many of these opening claims are not exactly perspicuous, at least for us. However, if we remain alive to certain key features pertaining to the philosophical landscape of Spinoza's times, his treatment of substance and mode starts to make sense. In fact, we will argue that he does not pack anything particularly controversial into his definitions. Here, as so often, two of Spinoza's most important philosophical sources make their presence felt: Descartes, who arguably was Spinoza's most influential predecessor, and the Aristotelian-scholastic tradition, which still dominated much of western thought in the seventeenth century.

As we have seen, a substance is "in itself," whereas a mode is an affection of a substance, which, according to Spinoza, means that a mode is "in another." The fundamental question would thus seem to be *what it means to be in itself or in another*. Here Spinoza offers us his understanding of the classic distinction between *substance* and *accident*. In the Aristotelian tradition, substances occupy a privileged ontological position: an accident is an entity that cannot exist on its own but needs something (ultimately a substance) to serve as a subject in which it exists; accidents are thus said to *inhere* in subjects, whereas substances are entities that *subsist*. Although scholastic debates concerning substances and different kinds of accidents are notoriously complicated, it is still possible to define the general difference between these concepts as follows: accidents are dependent on the substances in which they inhere, but substances are not similarly dependent on their accidents, nor do substances exist in subjects. For instance, blackness is an accident and can only exist in a substance, such as Bucephalus (the famous horse of Alexander the Great); Bucephalus itself, in contrast, does not exist in any other subject.[3] This line of thought is part and parcel of western thought, and nothing indicates that Spinoza would want to depart from it. Quite the contrary: the wording of 1def3 and 1def5 strongly echoes the following passage from Thomas Aquinas's *Summa Theologiae*

(I, 29.2, resp.): "[T]hose things subsist which exist in themselves, and not in another." Spinoza's "being in itself" and "being in another" would thus seem to track rather faithfully the traditional Aristotelian distinction between subsistence and inherence.

Much of the aforementioned scholastic framework can still be found in Descartes, who in the first part of the *Principles of Philosophy* discusses the meaning of fundamental ontological terms. Much attention has been directed to the fact that he starts by emphasizing the causal independence of substances in Proposition 51 – which is a point to which we will return later – but the governing assumption underpinning much of what Descartes says is that there are things, that is, substances, in which some other entities – he refers to them variably as attributes, qualities, modes, and properties – inhere. The following passages make this clear. First, the French version of the *Principles* contains a supplement to Proposition 51 in which Descartes notes that apart from substances, there are "qualities" or "attributes," which "are of such a nature that they cannot exist without other things" (CSM I, 210). Second, he claims that "we cannot initially become aware of a substance merely through its being an existing thing," but the presence of a substance can easily be inferred from the perception we have of some of the attributes the substance possesses (*Principles* I.52; CSM I, 210). Third, in his explication of what is meant by "modal distinction" (*Principles* I.61; CSM I, 214), Descartes notes that modes inhere in substances. Finally, in the Second Set of Replies to the *Meditations*, Descartes begins the definition of substance by saying that it is the term that "applies to every thing in which whatever we perceive immediately resides, as in a subject" (CSM II, 114).

Descartes's view can be expressed using the terms Spinoza later adopts by saying that modes and attributes inhere in substances. Modes are determining properties that are subject to change, whereas attributes are properties that remain constant during a finite substance's existence[4]; among the attributes, there is always one that is principal, which constitutes the substance's essence (*Principles* I.53; CSM I, 210). Interestingly, this part of the *Principles* suggests that Descartes adopts in many ways a non-Aristotelian framework for conceiving of substances, essences, and different kinds of (necessary and non-necessary) accidents.[5] Nevertheless, he accepts the traditional idea that modes or properties inhere in substances, whereas substances do not inhere in anything – they "need only the ordinary concurrence of God in order to exist" (*Principles* I.51, French edition; CSM I, 210).

When Spinoza says that substances are in themselves whereas modes are in another, he is thus respecting the traditional way of conceiving things and their properties. In this kind of ontology, there are those things, namely substances, that do not exist in anything else but are ontologically self-supporting. However, they always have some determining features, namely modes or modifications – Spinoza's gloss for accidents – that exist in, or inhere in, substances. Nothing more and nothing less is put forward at this stage. It is thus understandable that Spinoza takes himself to be entitled to hold, without offering any further proof, that modes are affections of substance (1def5). And as it is an axiom for him that "[w]hatever is, is either in itself or in another" (1a1), he feels entitled to arrive at the conclusion that "outside the intellect there is nothing except substances and their affections" (1p4d).[6] The only entities in Spinoza's ontology classifiable as *things* are substances and modes.

As noted above, the difference between substance and mode is delineated not only in terms of relations of inherence but also in terms of relations of conception. Substance is "conceived through itself" (1def3), while modes are conceived through something else (1def5). What, exactly, is at stake here? It seems that the way in which conceivability is treated in 1def3 and 1def5 reflects the Aristotelian view that substances have definitional priority over accidents: a definition reveals the essence of the thing defined, and the definition of an accident must refer to something other than the accident, namely the subject in which the accident in question inheres, whereas a substance is definable without reference to anything external to the substance.[7] So when Spinoza elucidates his claim that a substance is conceived through itself by saying that a substance's "concept does not require the concept of another thing, from which it must be formed" (1def3), he can be regarded as proceeding broadly along traditional lines.

Even if we grant that 1def3 and 1def5 echo certain Aristotelian doctrines, Descartes still seems to play a much more important role here.[8] The crucial passage reads:

A substance may indeed be known through any attribute at all; but each substance has one principal property which constitutes its nature and essence, and to which all its other properties are referred. Thus extension in length, breadth and depth constitutes the nature of corporeal substance; and thought constitutes the nature of thinking substance. Everything else which can be attributed to body presupposes extension, and is merely a mode of an extended thing; and similarly, whatever we find in the mind is simply one of the various modes of thinking. *For example, shape is unintelligible except in an extended thing; and motion is unintelligible except as motion in an extended space; while imagination, sensation and will are intelligible only in a thinking thing. By contrast, it is possible to understand extension without shape or movement, and thought without imagination or sensation, and so on;* and this is quite clear to anyone who gives the matter his attention. (*Principles* I.53; CSM I, 210–11, emphasis added)

In other words, no particular body or idea can be conceived without conceiving extension and thought, respectively.

In claiming that substances are conceived through themselves, and modes through another, Spinoza is just formulating in his own way the conceptual priority traditionally given to substances over properties. Spinoza's definitions of substance and mode, then, would have been relatively uncontroversial.[9] Substance (such as Bucephalus the horse) is a self-supporting and conceptually independent entity, while modes (such as blackness) inhere in and are conceived through their substance.[10] This means that all his radicalism notwithstanding, Spinoza can be said to operate within a time-honored framework.

2.2 Attribute

The third element that receives its own definition in the opening pages of the *Ethics*, that of attribute, completes Spinoza's basic ontology. He defines it as follows: "By attribute I understand what the intellect perceives of a substance, as constituting its essence" (1def4).

We can tentatively characterize attributes as *basic ways of being*.[11] The historical context of the concept is not hard to locate: the notion matches the Cartesian notion of principal attribute or property "which constitutes its [the substance's] nature and essence" (*Principles* I.53; CSM I, 210). For instance, to take a traditional example, as "human being" was traditionally defined as "rational animal," rationality and animality could be said to "constitute the essence" of any human being.[12] As a consequence, 1def4 would quite naturally be read as saying no more than that there are certain features that count as essential to a thing, features so fundamental to a substance that they make it what it is.

Here, however, perennial interpretative challenges concerning the substance–attribute relationship begin to crop up. To begin with, Spinoza claims in 1p10 and its scholium that attributes are conceived through themselves but that "each being must be conceived under some attribute" (1p10s). But if a substance must be conceived under some attribute, how can it also be conceived through itself? Here Spinoza seems to confer conceptual priority to attributes over substances, which conflicts with the preeminent and independent position just assigned to substances.

In order to make sense of this, we must dig deeper into what an attribute is. There have been two basic approaches to this problem, usually called the subjectivist and the objectivist readings. The subjectivist takes the attribute to be a mere way of grasping a substance, which introduces a strong element of mind-dependence. The objectivist, on the other hand, holds that the attributes are genuine mind-independent features of reality.

According to one prominent version of the objectivist reading, substances are identical with attributes.[13] This helps to solve the problem of how a substance can be conceived both through itself and through its attribute. There are also passages that taken at face value rather straightforwardly confirm this position: in 1p4d, for instance, Spinoza contends that "there is nothing outside the intellect through which a number of things can be distinguished from one another except substances, *or* what is the same (by def4), their attributes, and their affections." This approach, however, encounters the following problem: the claim of (numerical) identity is incompatible with the claim that "it is far from absurd to attribute many attributes to one substance" (1p10s). It seems that substances cannot be simply identified with attributes.

As for the subjectivist reading, Spinoza arguably invites it when he defines attributes as "what the intellect perceives of a substance, as [*tanquam*] constituting its essence" (1def4).[14] There would thus be no special problem in one substance having many attributes: one and the same object can of course be perceived in many different ways, and Spinoza's claim would simply be that there are certain basic ways in which a substance can be perceived, and he calls these basic ways attributes. However, the subjectivist reading is hard to square with the fact that, on the whole, Spinoza depicts attributes as something quite objective, real, or actual.[15]

It is worth observing that Spinoza shows at most a very mild concern about this issue that has vexed his readers for ages. The passage that is supposed to explain why it is "far from absurd to attribute many attributes to one substance" simply reads:

> From these propositions it is evident that although two attributes may be conceived to be really distinct (i.e., one may be conceived without the aid of the other), we still can not infer from that that they constitute two beings, *or* two different substances. For it is of the nature of a substance that each of its attributes is conceived through itself, since all the attributes it has have always been in it together, and one could not be produced by another, but each expresses the reality, *or* being of substance. (1p10s)

The propositions referred to in the beginning ("[f]rom these propositions it is evident") are presumably 1p9 and 1p10. The former contends that it is "evident from" the very definition of attribute that reality and being correlate with the number of attributes of a thing; the latter says that attributes are conceived through themselves. The foremost aim of 1p10s is obviously a negative one, namely to show that from the fact that attributes are really distinct it does not follow that each attribute must constitute a thing of its own. This is an important point, given the Cartesian doctrine that each substance can have only one principal attribute. Spinoza's idea here may well be as follows, as Michael Della Rocca (2002: 18, 28–9) has argued. No attribute, E, can offer grounds for a substance not to have some other attribute, T, because then a fact about T – that it is not possessed by a certain substance – would be explained by E, which would be for something concerning T to be conceived through E, which would be contrary to T's status as an attribute, as something that is conceived solely through itself. In other words, there is a *conceptual barrier* between attributes, which in this kind of case would be violated.

As we see it, the crucial scholium does not shed much positive light on our present question. Spinoza seems to think that just as we human beings are fundamentally both mental and physical creatures, a substance can be essentially both thinking and extended – thought and extension being the only attributes *we* are acquainted with (2p1–p2).[16] However, it is difficult to see why any dedicated Cartesian would be especially impressed by the argument of 1p10s. And indeed, the general problems that we have considered concerning the nature of attributes continue to puzzle scholars to this day.

2.3 Monism

Thus far, we have seen that Spinoza adheres quite closely to a traditional line of thought with regard to the concepts of substance and mode: substance is a self-supporting and conceptually independent entity, and modes inhere in and are conceived through their substance. Attribute is defined in a Cartesian fashion, as that which constitutes the essence of a substance; but Spinoza departs from Descartes in asserting that one substance can have many attributes. In general, Spinoza's strategy is to adopt fairly uncontroversial metaphysical starting points, from which he then proceeds, in geometrical fashion, to derive stronger and more surprising conclusions. There is little doubt that *monism*, the thesis that there is only one substance, is the most radical and important of those conclusions.

Spinoza's argument for monism is rooted in a claim he makes about the substance–attribute relation: "In nature there cannot be two or more substances of the same nature *or* attribute" (1p5). This much-discussed proposition receives a detailed demonstration:

> If there were two or more distinct substances, they would have to be distinguished from one another either by a difference in their attributes, or by a difference in their affections (by p4). If only by a difference in their attributes, then it will be conceded that there is only one of the same attribute. But if by a difference in their affections, then since a substance is prior in nature to its affections (by p1), if the affections are put to one side and [the substance] is considered in itself, i.e. (by def3 and a6), considered truly, one cannot be conceived to be distinguished from another, i.e. (by p4), there cannot be many, but only one [of the same nature *or* attribute]. (1p5d)

Spinoza seems here to be relying on a version of the *identity of indiscernibles* that came to be closely associated with Leibniz. According to the identity of indiscernibles, if there is no feature with regard to which two objects differ from each other, they must be identical; conversely, any two distinct objects must be distinguished by some (intrinsic) quality. Attributes and modes are the only candidates for entities that can be used to distinguish substances from each other. Spinoza suggests that affections or modes cannot do the job of distinguishing substances since, once again, substances are prior to modes. Distinguishing a substance by its modes would entail that the substance would be conceived through a mode, which is contrary to the very definitions of substance and mode.

So two substances cannot be individuated by their modes, and we are left with attributes to do the job. Spinoza remarks that if substances were distinguished "only by a difference in their attributes, then it will be conceded that there is only one of the same attribute." One way of understanding the claim here is that if substance x is distinguished from substance y by the fact that the former has attribute E and the latter has attribute T, then it will be admitted that the two substances do not share attributes. Perhaps Spinoza also means to suggest here that if we take any attribute, say E, it is evident that if both substance x and substance y have E, it cannot be E that differentiates x and y from each other; thus, given the identity of indiscernibles, x and y must be identical. Any putative case of attribute sharing between two distinct substances is on closer inspection a case of substance identity – and so Spinoza thinks that he can confidently assert that no two or more substances can have the same attribute.

Here, however, Spinoza appears to be on less solid ground than with regard to modes: the argument seems to go through only if we assume that substances cannot have more than one attribute. For if substances can have more than one attribute, then, as commentators as far back as Leibniz have objected, why could not x and y share E and differ with regard to some other attributes, so that x would have E and T, y have E and Z? There would, then, be a way to distinguish x from y based on their attributes even though they shared E, and this would undermine Spinoza's argument, which would be valid only on the assumption that substances have only a single attribute; but, as we have seen, Spinoza allows that a substance can have many attributes.

There is, however, a recently presented argument in Spinoza's defense, the starting point of which is that Spinoza accepts the claim that "[e]ach attribute of a substance, independently of any other attribute of that substance, is sufficient for conceiving of that substance."[17] This claim, which seems plausible enough in the Spinozistic framework, entails that there cannot be cases in which, for instance, x has E and T, and y has E and Z, for then x could not be conceived solely through E, that is, as the substance that has E, because this would not be sufficient to distinguish x from y. Instead, x would have to be conceived as the substance with E *and* T, and this would mean that the concept of a certain substance with E would require not only the concept of E but also the concept of T, and would thus be partly conceived through *T*. But this would violate the above-mentioned conceptual barrier between the attributes: conceiving a substance with a certain attribute would depend on conceiving some other attribute. Thus the conceptual independence of attributes could rule out this objection.

Still, even if we grant all of this, it should be noted that it has not yet even been established whether *any* of the aforementioned entities – substances, modes, or attributes – really exist.[18] Claims concerning what there is and what human beings are appear only when Spinoza connects the notions of substance, attribute, and mode with causal notions, which – strikingly – are missing from 1def3–def5. Here we see his unique philosophical system quickly begin to take shape.

The seventh proposition of the opening part of the *Ethics* makes the crucial existential claim concerning substances and can serve as a vantage point from which to examine the way in which Spinoza moves from purely conceptual considerations to existential ones. The proposition states, "[i]t pertains to the nature of a substance to exist (1p7)," and it is proved as follows: "A substance cannot be produced by anything else (by p6c); therefore it will be the cause of itself, i.e. (by def1), its essence necessarily involves existence, *or* it pertains to its nature to exist" (1p7d). The argument here may be construed in two different ways, corresponding to the two ways in which 1p6c – the corollary stating the causal independence of substances – can be demonstrated. We will follow the quicker route, which is the more interesting one for our purposes[19]; according to it, adding the following axiom to the notion of substance is all that is needed to show that a substance is *causa sui*, cause of itself: "The knowledge of an effect depends on, and involves, the knowledge of its cause" (1a4).

This axiom enables Spinoza to argue that if a substance had an external cause, it would be conceived through that cause; and this would violate the claim of 1def3 since a substance cannot be produced by anything else. It is thus, according to Spinoza, the cause of itself. There is, then, an exceedingly quick route from the conceptual independence of substances to a fundamental causal claim.[20] If conceiving things requires conceiving their causes (as 1a4 says), everything conceptually independent must be causally self-sufficient.

The obvious and often repeated objection to 1p7 is that even if a substance cannot be produced by anything external to it, it does not follow that it necessarily exists – it only follows that *if* a substance exists, the cause of that existence must lie within it. Here Spinoza seems to rely on the *principle of sufficient reason*, according to which everything must have a cause or reason, as he reasons that because each thing must be brought about either by external causes or by itself, and because in the case of a substance external causes are ruled out, the only option is that it is self-caused, which, by 1def1, means that it must exist by its own essence. Still, this leaves open whether there are things with such essences – most importantly, whether or not there is a God that satisfies the strictures of substancehood.

Spinoza gives his answer to these questions when he demonstrates the claim that "God, *or* a substance consisting of infinite attributes, each of which expresses eternal and infinite essence, necessarily exists" (1p11). The second demonstration begins by maintaining, "[f]or each thing there must be assigned a cause, *or* reason, as much for its existence as for its nonexistence." In other words, there must be a sufficient reason not only for the *existence* but also for the *nonexistence* of anything.[21] That reason, Spinoza continues, must be located either inside or outside of the thing in question, and because in the case of God – who is a substance and as such causally isolated – it cannot be outside of it, the reason for the existence or nonexistence of God must be found in God's essence. Now, the only possible reason for the latter would be that God's essence is contradictory, like that of a square circle; and because this cannot be, God's essence can only be the cause or reason for God's existence. Given this, we can be certain that at least God as substance necessarily exists.

Hence, if granted certain additional premises, Spinoza has succeeded in covering the distance from mere conceptual considerations to contentions concerning real existence. The claim of 1p11, that God necessarily exists, was of course a cornerstone of traditional philosophical theology, so there is nothing extraordinary in that. Moreover, we have seen that Spinoza has been working with a notion of substance that is conceptually quite close to the traditional one. So far, so good. But then Spinoza, very quickly, develops his argument to a direction that leads to a collision of the greatest magnitude with traditional philosophical theology: "Except God, no substance can be or be conceived" (1p14). Here is the argument:

Since God is an absolutely infinite being, of whom no attribute which expresses an essence of substance can be denied (by def6), and he necessarily exists (by p11), if there were any substance except God, it would have to be explained through some attribute of God, and so two substances of the same attribute would exist, which (by p5) is absurd. And so except God, no substance can be or, consequently, be conceived. For if it could be conceived, it would have to be conceived as existing. But this (by the first part of this demonstration) is absurd. Therefore, except for God no substance can be or be conceived. (1p14d)

In other words, since God, the substance with all the attributes, necessarily exists and as substances cannot share attributes (1p5), there can be no other substances besides God.[22]

From the claim that there is only one substance, it is – given Spinoza's understanding of substance and mode – only a stone's throw to the monistic credo, "[w]hatever is, is in God, and nothing can be or be conceived without God" (1p15). Spinoza consistently endorses monism throughout his philosophical career. For instance, in the *Short Treatise* he proclaims, "Nature consists of infinite attributes, of which each is perfect in its kind. This agrees perfectly with the definition one gives of God" (KV II.12). Indeed, this linchpin of Spinoza's thought may well have been a major reason why he was excommunicated. He seems to have come to endorse it years before his earliest extant writings.

Spinoza's overall argumentative strategy in the beginning of his magnum opus can thus be described as follows: he begins with relatively uncontentious – or at least not easily rejectable – definitions and axioms and then, within the span of a handful of propositions, draws momentous conclusions from them, ending up with a position strongly at odds both with theological orthodoxy and with the dominant received philosophical worldview. According to Spinoza's position, given that there is but one substance, God or the whole of Nature, all finite entities usually regarded as substances – such as horses, tables, planets, and, most importantly, human beings – undergo an unprecedented repositioning of their ontological status: they are demoted from substances to modes of the one substance. In his correspondence, Spinoza develops a particularly memorable analogue of the human condition:

> Let us feign now, if you please, that there is a little worm living in the blood which is capable of distinguishing by sight the particles of the blood, of lymph, of chyle, etc. [...] Indeed, it would live in this blood as we do in this part of the universe, and would consider each particle of the blood as a whole, not as a part. [...] Now all bodies in nature can and must be conceived as we have here conceived the

blood, for all bodies are surrounded by others[.] [...] Every body [...] must be considered as a part of the whole universe[.] And [...] the nature of the universe is not limited, as the nature of the blood is, but is absolutely infinite[.] (Ep. 32; G IV, 171–3)

Spinoza's point is clear: in our everyday lives we conceive of our surroundings as if its inhabitants, human beings included, were wholes (that is, substances) independent of each other – and in this respect we are just as mistaken as is the little worm that considers particles of blood as separate wholes.

2.4 Necessitarianism

A puzzle remains concerning how exactly we are to conceive of finite things as modes of God. It is beyond doubt that *some* kind of causal relation obtains between God-substance and its modes[23]; and based on the preceding discussion, it is also evident that finite modes inhere in God (1p15).[24] The fundamental proposition, as important as it is intriguing, describes the relationship as follows:

> From the necessity of the divine nature there must follow infinitely many things in infinitely many modes (i.e., everything which can fall under an infinite intellect). (1p16).

> This proposition must be plain to anyone, provided he attends to the fact that *the intellect infers from the given definition of any thing a number of properties that really do follow necessarily from it (i.e., from the very essence of the thing)*; and that it infers more properties the more the definition of the thing expresses reality, i.e., the more reality the essence of the defined thing involves. But since the divine nature has absolutely infinite attributes (by def6), each of which also expresses an essence infinite in its own kind, from its necessity there must follow infinitely many things in infinite modes (i.e., everything which can fall under an infinite intellect). (1p16d, emphasis added)

The discussion of the previous sections allows us to unpack the idea rather quickly. Spinoza begins by presupposing that each and every genuine thing, including God, has its own particular *essence* (or nature)[25] that constitutes the thing. The essence is thoroughly intelligible and can be perfectly captured by a *definition*. Both the essence and the definition have a certain structure: from the definition certain *properties* (for Spinoza, modes) can be inferred, and this expresses those things that necessarily follow from – are realized by – the essence in question. This is in line with the fact that, over time, the *essence–property ontology* had come to be seen in increasingly robust causal terms, making essences causally productive of their properties. A traditional example of this would be the way that the essence of fire was thought to cause heat.

Thus what drives the argument is a variant of a feature widely endorsed in western thought; but Spinoza's approach has two notable peculiarities. First, he considers essence–property ontology to apply to, and indeed reveal, the way in which *God* produces infinitely many things as modes.[26] Second, he believes that *geometrical objects* reveal in an exemplary fashion this inner structure of things: Spinoza famously states that an infinity of things follow from God's essence "by the same necessity and in the same way" (1p17s) as the property of having internal angles that are equal to two right angles follows from the essence of a triangle. Indeed, we should be clear as to where Spinoza's radicalism lies: not in the claim that the essence–property relationship is a causal one or that geometrical objects necessarily have certain properties but in the application of these features to the relationship between God and finite things.[27]

An examination of Spinoza's view of divine causation reveals the grounds for his necessitarianism, namely the doctrine that nothing could happen in any other way than it actually does. To put things bluntly, Spinoza's idea here is as follows: because all finite things (and their activities) are properties that follow from God's essence, just like the property of fulfilling the Pythagorean theorem follows from the essence of a right triangle, any difference in what happens in the world would require that God have a different essence, which is impossible. This captures the way in which Spinoza defends the claim that "[t]hings could have been produced by God in no other way, and in no other order than they have been produced" (1p33):

> For all things have necessarily followed from God's given nature (by p16), and have been determined from the necessity of God's nature to exist and produce an effect in a certain way (by p29). Therefore, if things could have been of another nature, or could have been determined to produce an effect in another way, so that the order of Nature was different, then God's nature could also have been other than it is now, and therefore (by p11) that [other nature] would also have had to exist, and consequently, there could have been two or more Gods, which is absurd (by p14c1). So things could have been produced in no other way and no other order, etc. (1p33d)

One might think that this cannot be right since we can full well conceive of non-actualized possibilities, like the French Revolution happening in 1787 instead of 1789. However, Spinoza insists that the mere fact that we can imagine something does not entail that it is metaphysically possible. In fact, belief in contingent things is, according to Spinoza, a confused product of our limited cognitive capacities:

> [A] thing is called contingent only because of a defect of our knowledge. For if we do not know that the thing's essence involves a contradiction, or if we do know very well that its essence does not involve a contradiction, and nevertheless can affirm nothing certainly about its existence, because the order of causes is hidden from us, it can never seem to us either necessary or impossible. So we call it contingent or possible. (1p33s1)

To summarize: no thing, not even God, can exist without certain necessary properties. A change in these properties would require a change in the fundamental nature of the thing in question. Hence nothing whatsoever could have been otherwise; or, to put the same thing differently, the actual world is the only possible world.[28] As we will see later on, this claim has momentous ramifications for the way in which Spinoza understands human freedom.

2.5 Subverting the tradition from within

We have argued that Spinoza's basic metaphysics relies on features of the western philosophical tradition, but that on the basis of this framework he subverts many tenets held dear by that same tradition. The definitions of substance, attribute, and mode are formulated in a somewhat peculiar manner, but they are nevertheless firmly rooted in the Aristotelian and Cartesian substance–property ontologies. Proceeding by way of certain innovations concerning the relationship between substance and attribute, Spinoza then arrives at his *monism*, in which the things around us are not only effects but modes of the single substance, namely God or Nature, that inhere in that substance and cannot be properly conceived apart from it. This applies to human beings as well, who relate to their surroundings much as a worm living in a bloodstream: like the worm, we are prone to mistake parts of the whole for independent entities. This philosophical worldview was, for Spinoza's contemporaries, deeply disturbing; but for many present-day readers, the idea that we all are part of a vast nature, thoroughly integrated to an infinite universe, is likely to strike a deep chord. This is probably especially true for scientifically minded thinkers: it is not by mistake that Einstein confessed that he believed in "Spinoza's God" – God stripped of all anthropomorphism.

Another major feature of the philosophical tradition Spinoza makes full use of is the idea that each thing is endowed with an essence that grounds a certain array of properties. Based on this essence–property ontology, Spinoza argues that God or Nature produces, by its nature, an infinity of properties (i.e., modes). This is certainly a bold move but one completely in line with Spinoza's naturalism: as God is a natural entity, indeed the whole of Nature itself, why would it not have the same kind of ontological structure that all natural things have? In fact, it is more striking that Spinoza treats the essence–property ontology in a geometrical key, from which he derives a uniquely strong version of necessitarianism: nothing could have been otherwise any more than a triangle could have angles summing to something else than two right angles. This contention is certainly something many people would want to resist: the libertarian position, according to which at least for the most part we can freely choose between different courses of action, still arguably constitutes the commonsense view. But let us postpone judgment about this until we have seen, in chapters to come, what Spinoza's alternative view of human action looks like.

Further reading

Bennett, Jonathan. 1984. *A Study of Spinoza's Ethics*. Cambridge: Cambridge University Press, chs 3–5.

Carriero, John. 1995. "On the Relationship between Mode and Substance in Spinoza's Metaphysics." *Journal of the History of Philosophy* 33(2): 245–73.

Della Rocca, Michael. 2008. *Spinoza*. London: Routledge, ch. 2.

Garrett, Don. 2018. *Nature and Necessity in Spinoza's Philosophy*. Oxford: Oxford University Press, chs 2–4.

Hübner, Karolina. 2016. "Spinoza on Essences, Universals, and Beings of Reason." *Pacific Philosophical Quarterly* 97(1): 58–88.

Lin, Martin. 2019. *Being and Reason: An Essay on Spinoza's Metaphysics*. Oxford: Oxford University Press.

Melamed, Yitzhak Y. 2013. *Spinoza's Metaphysics: Substance and Thought*. Oxford: Oxford University Press.

Viljanen, Valtteri. 2011. *Spinoza's Geometry of Power*. Cambridge: Cambridge University Press, chs 1–3.

3

Religion

In the last chapter, we saw that for Spinoza: there is one substance, God or Nature; "nothing can be or be conceived without God" (1p15); everything that exists is caused by, and is conceptually dependent on, God (1p18d); and the actual causal order of things is the only possible order of things (1p33). The two central doctrines of the opening part of the *Ethics* – monism and necessaritarianism – are bold metaphysical positions, even by today's standards. But to express these views, and to apply the label "God" to the one substance, in seventeenth-century Europe was to open oneself wide up to the charge of blasphemy. After all, God was traditionally seen as transcendent, decidedly distinct from his creation, and the identification of God with Nature denied that distinction, making him immanent to the world. Given this account, Spinoza's decision not to publish the *Ethics* in his lifetime was prudent. Nevertheless, he did not intend to erode all forms of religious belief. Rather, in the *Ethics* he sought to advance a rational theology that would capture the core of religious belief, engendering a love of the one true cause of all things. And in the *Theological-Political Treatise*, he sought to liberate people from superstitious forms of religion that keep them locked in fear and hatred. In distinct ways, in these two very different works, Spinoza sought to supplant traditional theology with a revisionary alternative, the core of which consisted in the promotion of love and of freedom of mind. Spinoza is not merely a critic of ordinary religion but also a profound – if profoundly unorthodox – religious thinker.

The structure of this chapter on Spinoza's religious thought will be as follows. We will begin by discussing some of the main problems encountered by traditional philosophical theology, followed by a sketch of some of the general ways that philosophers sought to overcome these problems. We will then explore Spinoza's revisionary theology, seeing why he thinks that his rational alternative preserves God's omnipotence better than alternatives, while avoiding other theological quandaries. Next, we explore his more pointed attack on revelation and scriptural interpretation in the TTP and consider how it fits into the larger polemical aims of the work. As Spinoza sees it, orthodox theology is not only philosophically bankrupt, it is potentially politically destabilizing, especially when clerics are accorded civic power. Consequently, the TTP is structured with the aim of diminishing clerical power. Ultimately, we see that the philosophical theology presented in the *Ethics* and in the TTP seeks to liberate humans from ignorance and hatred and to promote mutual support, freedom of philosophizing, and love of God.

3.1 Traditional philosophical theology

Traditional philosophical theology takes as foundational the view that God is omniscient, omnipotent, and good. Let us briefly consider each of these features. To claim that God is omniscient or all-knowing is not to say that God knows the entire course of events in the way that I know that my cat is crying. I know that my cat is crying because I perceive his plaintive calls. But God's knowledge is not receptive in this way; it is in some sense productive. Things come about as they do in part *because* he knows them. Still, since God's *intellect* comprehends even nonexistent thing (e.g., centaurs, unicorns) and possible, but non-actual, sets of events (e.g., Caesar turning back at the Rubicon), if we are to understand why things are the way that they are, we must appeal not merely to God's intellect but also to his *will*. Like his intellect, his will is infinite – that is, there is nothing that is genuinely possible, nothing that falls under his intellect, that he could not will into existence. There is obviously a tight connection between God's will and his intellect as they conspire to determine what gets created. However, on this traditional conception, there is a clear difference between God's will and his intellect since he does not will all that he understands.

This brings us to the third feature mentioned above: God's *goodness*, as manifest through his providence. Though his will is infinite, his intellect directs his will, supplying reasons for acting.

Specifically, God directs the order of nature in accordance with his apprehension of what is good, taking special concern for his most beloved creation: human beings. These features – omniscience, omnipotence, and goodness – were central to the general conception of God that served as the foundation of philosophical theology in the medieval and modern periods.

But there is a fundamental tension between God's will and intellect in traditional philosophical theology. It seems that there are certain eternal truths that even God grasps *as necessary and immutable*, such as the fact that two and two make four. Perhaps there are also moral features of the world that obtain independently of God's will. After all, in claiming that he is providential, one is claiming that he acts for reasons, that he apprehends the superiority of one set of things or events over another, which explains why he wills it. If that is right, then it would seem that there is an objective moral standard that God understands and looks to in determining his will. Indeed, to deny that there are moral standards that exist independently of God's will and to insist instead that anything that God does – even if it includes tormenting the innocent – is good simply because he wills it seems to undercut the view of God as provident or benevolent, rendering his actions normatively arbitrary. However, to admit that there is a moral order that exists independently of God's will would be to allow that there are things that lie beyond God's power and that God's will is in fact in a sense limited by extrinsic moral laws or principles. It would seem that something has to give: either God is not really good or he is not all-powerful since his will is being constrained by a moral order.

This is a variation on the Euthyphro dilemma, named after the Platonic dialogue in which the eponymous character is challenged by Socrates to consider whether certain things are pious simply because the gods love them or whether the gods love these things because they are themselves pious. In the medieval and modern periods, philosophers and theologians wrestled with a variant of this puzzle. Those who stressed that there really is a moral order that God grasps intellectually came to be referred to as *Intellectualists* (or Realists), while those who emphasized the boundlessness of God's will, even in determining what counts as good, came to be known as *Voluntarists*. In what follows, we will explore the views of Intellectualists and Voluntarists in a bit more depth before turning to Spinoza's attack on the very foundation of traditional philosophical theology.

The most prominent and influential medieval Intellectualist was Thomas Aquinas (1225–1274). Aquinas held that the will and the intellect are both part of the divine essence.[1] However, God's understanding encompasses more than what he wills. God has practical knowledge of those things that he creates, such as lemon trees, lichens, and lemurs. But he also has speculative knowledge of things that are possible but non-actual, like griffins and World Cup championships won by the Finnish Men's National Soccer Team. Practical knowledge alone involves the will: "[A] form considered by the intellect does not move or cause anything except through the will, whose object is the end and the good, by which someone is moved to act. Hence, the speculative intellect does not move" (*Summa contra Gentiles* I.72.6).

As there are things that God knows only speculatively, but not practically, God's will does not extend to all that he knows. Moreover, even those things that God wills into existence have a specific nature or essence that gives them the powers and qualities that they have: "[A] saw, because it is made of iron, must be hard; and a man [because he is rational] is necessarily capable of learning" (*Summa contra Gentiles* II.30.11). While some other philosophers thought that God's will is the direct and immediate source of all causal powers in the world, such that if iron is hard in any particular instance it is because God directly wills that this is so, Aquinas believed that God created things with real natures that have genuinely causal properties, preserving the commonsense view that the saw cuts the wood because it is made of iron, and iron, by its nature, is harder than wood.

Natures or essences also play a crucial role in Thomistic ethics. Aquinas maintains that things are good insofar as they enable one to perfect one's nature and thereby contribute to one's happiness. Things are not good for humans simply because God commands them; rather, the good is inscribed into our very natures. However, by insisting that God's will extends only to a part of God's knowledge and that there is a structure to the world – i.e., things have real natures and are causally productive without God's continuous, direct intervention – Aquinas is susceptible to the objection that he limits God's power since if God were truly omnipotent, there would be no fixed natural or moral order to the world. Everything would depend on the divine will. To save God's omnipotence, Aquinas appeals to two conceptions of God's power: God's absolute power (*potentia Dei absoluta*) and God's ordained power (*potentia Dei ordinate*). The latter refers to the power that is expressed in the actual order of created things. But this does not exhaust God's absolute power, which encompasses all that is in God's intellect – his speculative as well as his practical knowledge. So, when we say that say that God is just or good, we are referring to his power as it is expressed in the order of created things. But when we say that God can do anything – or at least anything that is logically possible – we are appealing to God's absolute power, which is in some sense prior to his actual decrees.

Aquinas's views were opposed by William of Ockham (c. 1287–1347). Ockham accepted the distinction between God's absolute and ordained power. But while Aquinas conceived of these as two different kinds of power – the power of God prior to exercising his will, and the power of God as expressed in his creation – Ockham regards these as two different aspects of a single power. The significance of this is that, on Ockham's account, God's absolute power is always available; he is never bound in any way, not even by his own decrees. As he baldly puts it, "God is under obligation to no one."[2] Ockham's staunch Voluntarism helps to explain another doctrine for which he is well known, namely, denial of the existence of universal forms or essences. For Ockham, to exist is to be a particular; universals – like "human" – are nothing but abstractions or mere names (this view is thus known as "nominalism"). Voluntarism supports nominalism since if God also retains his absolute power, he cannot be said to have created fixed, general essences. Ockham's Voluntarism extends to moral propositions, all of which are contingent on God's will. Nothing is necessarily good or evil. Things are made good and evil simply because God wills them to be the case. A couple of centuries later, Protestant reformer John Calvin (1509–1564) would endorse a quite similar view – a view with which Spinoza would have been very familiar, as Calvinist theology dominated Dutch intellectual life in his time. The obvious problem confronting Voluntarists like Ockham and Calvin is that that they render God's will arbitrary and thereby seem to deprive him of moral goodness.

Debates between Intellectualists and Voluntarists continued in the modern era. Descartes sought to find out a middle way between the two positions. He appears to side with Intellectualists in positing the existence of "true and immutable natures," from which various properties can be deduced.[3] For instance, it pertains to the nature of a triangle that its interior angles add up to two right angles. However, the claim that there are immutable natures or eternal truths struck some readers as implying that even God himself could not change these natures. Pierre Gassendi raised such a challenge in the Fifth Set of Objections to the *Meditations*, to which Descartes replied:

> You say that you think it is "very hard" to propose that there is anything immutable and eternal apart from God. You would be right to think this if I was talking about existing things, or if I was proposing something as immutable in the sense that its immutability was independent of God. But just as the poets suppose that the Fates were originally established by Jupiter, but that after they were established he bound himself to abide by them, so I do not think that the essences of things, and the mathematical truths which we can know concerning them, are independent of God. Nevertheless I do think that they are immutable and eternal, since the will and decree of God willed and decreed that they should be so. (CSM II, 261)

This attempted compromise did not satisfy Descartes's friend Marin Mersenne, who in the Sixth Set of Objections challenged him to make clear how there could be eternal, necessary truths, that depend on God's will. Descartes's response reveals his eagerness to defend the total dependence of all things – including truths concerning good and evil – on God's will:

> If anyone attends to the immeasurable greatness of God he will find it manifestly clear that there can be nothing whatsoever which does not depend on him. This applies not just to everything that subsists, but to all order, every law, and every reason for anything's being true or good. [...] If some reason for something's being good had existed prior to his preordination, this would have determined God to prefer those things which it was best to do. But on the contrary, just because he resolved to prefer those things which are now to be done, for this very reason, in the words of Genesis, "they are very good"; in other words, the reason for their goodness depends on the fact that he exercised his will to make them so. (CSM II, 293–4)

Descartes concedes, however, that it is bound to be "unintelligible" to humans how God "could have brought it about from eternity that it was not true that twice four make eight, and so on" (CSM II, 294). But we know that he could have, given his unfettered will. Like Aquinas and others who allowed for fixed created natures, Descartes was quite anxious to show *that* his account was compatible with God's omnipotence, even while he concedes that he cannot show *how* it is compatible.

This is not the only time that Descartes seems to just shrug off an apparent inconsistency. In his *Principles of Philosophy* (I.39–41; CSM I, 205–6), Descartes asserts that "[t]he freedom of the will is self-evident," declaring that it is "among the first and most common notions that are innate in us." However, he then proceeds to assert that "[i]t is also certain that everything was preordained by God," advising against trying to reconcile these claims since it will only get us "into great difficulties," as this is a matter on which "we cannot get a sufficient grasp." We get a sense of the tangle that Descartes sought to bypass by returning to Aquinas. Aquinas sought to reconcile God's certain knowledge of all things with future contingent events, like those that depend on human (free) will, by claiming that, while God knows all that will happen, he knows future contingent events not *as* future since he grasps all moments in time at once. This raises significant problems since God is not simply supposed to *learn* what happens; his knowledge is, as noted above, supposed to be causal. If his knowledge is dependent on the actions of others, it is hard to see how one could defend his omnipotence. We may call this *the problem of human freedom*.

In addition to the aforementioned puzzles about how to reconcile God's goodness with his omnipotence and how to square human freedom with divine foreknowledge, traditional philosophical theology is also dogged by the so-called *problem of evil*: how can an omnipotent and perfect God admit the presence of evils (e.g., slavery and genocide). The existence of evil seems to reveal that God either lacks the power to prevent such suffering or is not all-loving. A straightforward response is that genuine evil is the product of free human choices. But this only brings us back to the problem of human freedom, while leaving unanswered why innocent people routinely suffer from ills like natural disasters and diseases that are not caused by human decisions. We see from this that traditional philosophical theology – with its distinction between the divine intellect and divine will and its commitment to God's omniscience, omnipotence, and goodness – is plagued by some rather serious and enduring challenges.

3.2 Critique of traditional philosophical theology

Spinoza's response to the problems with traditional philosophical theology is to reject the very premise that generates much of the trouble, namely, the view that God's will is distinct from his (or its) intellect. On his account, to separate God's intellect and will would be to destroy God's unity, to sever Nature in two. As we have seen, there are also reasons to think that it would deprive God of omnipotence. Spinoza seeks to preserve God's unity and omnipotence where traditional alternatives fail. Spinoza's engagement with traditional philosophical theology in the *Ethics* is most apparent in two key propositions and their attendant corollaries and scholia: 1p17 and 1p33.

In 1p17, Spinoza asserts: "God acts from the laws of his nature alone and is compelled by no one." And he makes it clear in the subsequent discussion that he intends this as an affirmation of divine omnipotence and as a rebuke of Intellectualism. When he claims that there is "no cause, either extrinsically or intrinsically, which prompts God to action" (1p17c1) and that God is therefore a "free cause" (1p17c2), according to his definition of a free thing as that "which exists from the necessity of its nature alone, and is determined to act by itself alone" (1def7), he is rejecting the notion that God's power is in any way limited. In the subsequent scholium, he sets out to refute traditional theology more generally, flatly denying that the intellect or the will "pertain to God's nature" (1p17s). He then targets Voluntarists, who conceive of God's "freedom" as the ability not to produce that which follows from his nature, which "is the same as if they were to say that God can bring it about that it would not follow from the nature of a triangle that its three angles are equal to two right angles; *or* that from a given cause the effect would not follow – which is absurd" (1p17s). He might have added that the view that God's power allows him to *prevent* things from following from his nature is absurd since the non-production of effects is a privation, not a power (1p11d3).

Later in the same scholium, Spinoza turns his attention once again to those Intellectualists who "do not believe that [God] can bring it about that all the things he actually understands exist" because "if he had created all the things in his intellect (they say), then he would have been able to create nothing more, which they believe to be incompatible with God's omnipotence" (1p17s). Against this view, Spinoza asserts that his conception of God better preserves God's power since on this view God creates everything that is genuinely possible, rendering God's power fully actual.[4] It is his opponents who limit God's power:

> [T]hey are forced to confess that God understands infinitely many creatable things, which nevertheless he will never be able to create.

For otherwise, if he created everything he understood [NS: to be creatable] he would (according to them) exhaust his omnipotence and render himself imperfect. Therefore to maintain that God is perfect, they are driven to maintain at the same time that he cannot bring about everything to which his power extends. I do not see what could be feigned which would be more absurd than this or more contrary to God's omnipotence. (1p17s)

By separating God's will from his intellect and claiming that God wills only some of what he understands, traditional philosophical theologians – particularly the Intellectualists – restrict God's causal power, assigning to God's intellect unrealized potentiality.

As for the distinction between God's absolute and God's ordained power, Spinoza will have no truck with it, laying into the traditional philosophical theologian in the second scholium to 1p33. To assign to God an absolute power, apart from the ordained power, by which God *could* theoretically alter his decrees, would be, once again, to split God's nature in two. One who insists that God still *could* have willed otherwise, Spinoza responds: "How would this be different from saying openly that God, who necessarily understands what he wills, can bring it about by his will that he understands things in another way than he does understand them?" (1p33s2).

On Spinoza's account, God's power is expressed in the eternal decrees that fix the actual order of nature; God's absolute power *is* God's ordained power, as it were. This preserves God's omnipotence better than the view that God possesses power that he does not use.

Ultimately, as Spinoza sees it, we must reject the view that will and intellect are distinct faculties that pertain to God's essence. Rather, on his account, will and intellect are particular modes of thinking (1p32d) that are "related to God's nature as motion and rest are" and "must be determined to exist and produce an effect in a certain way" (1p32c2). Near the end of the second part of the *Ethics*, he sheds further light on the relationship between will and intellect, claiming that an act of volition is not distinct from an act of thinking (2p49). Rather, volitions are intrinsic to ideas, just as motion and rest is intrinsic to bodies. As he straightforwardly asserts, "[t]he will and the intellect are one and the same" (2p49c). Spinoza's positive view of will and intellect is comprised of three main claims: (1) will and intellect are particular modes of thinking, i.e., volitions and ideas; (2) as particular modes of thinking, they are necessitated; (3) volitions and ideas are one and the same thing.[5] While the resulting picture is quite unorthodox, Spinoza thinks that it captures the core of traditional philosophical theology since it preserves God's omniscience – as God's intellect comprises everything that exists or is intelligible – and, as we have seen, God's omnipotence.

Spinoza's account gets around the problem of human freedom and the problem of evil by rejecting the accounts of freedom and evaluative predicates that give rise to the problems in the first place, offering revisionary alternatives in their place. With respect to freedom, he flatly denies that human beings or anything else are free in the sense of not being determined by the laws of nature.[6] However, Spinoza does admit that humans can achieve a degree of freedom, if we understand this in terms of one's ability to produce effects from one's own nature alone.[7] And this notion of freedom is perfectly compatible with the account of divine omniscience and omnipotence described above.[8] For this reason, Spinoza thinks that he can sidestep the problem of human freedom.

Spinoza avoids the so-called problem of evil by denying the objective reality of evil itself. In the appendix to *Ethics* part 1, he claims that evaluative concepts like "good" and "evil" are really just "modes of imagining, and do not indicate the nature of anything" (1app; G II, 83). While judgments of good and evil purport to be about objects themselves, what they really express is the condition of the perceiver. Absolutely speaking, nothing is good or evil in itself. Near the end of the appendix to *Ethics* part 1, Spinoza considers the problem of evil: "For many are accustomed to arguing in this way: if all things have followed from the necessity of God's most perfect nature, why are there so many imperfections in Nature? why are things corrupt to the point where they stink? so ugly that they produce nausea? why is there confusion, evil, and sin?" (1app; G II, 83).

He thinks that such questions are based on two false assumptions: (1) that conditions like evil, corruption, ugliness, disorder, and imperfection are objective features of the world itself rather than "beings of imagination"; and, (2) that God acts with an end in view, specifically, the benefit of humanity. While we will later see that Spinoza does want to preserve a meaningful sense in which we can assess things as good and evil in relationship to us,[9] the point that he stresses here is that good and evil are not features of things in themselves and that God does not act for the sake of any end. As he puts it earlier, "all things have been predetermined by God, not from freedom of the will or absolute good pleasure, but from God's absolute nature, or infinite power" (1app; G II, 77).

At this point, the revisionary implications of Spinoza's philosophical theology can be fully appreciated. On his account, once
we properly understand what God's omniscience and omnipotence consist in, we are led to abandon the third main feature in
the traditional conception of God: his goodness or providence.
We see this in Spinoza's critique of Intellectualists, who claim that
"[God] does all things for the sake of the good" and thus "seem to
place something outside of God, which does not depend on God,
to which God attends, as a model, in what he does, and at which
he aims, as at a certain goal. This is simply to subject God to fate"
(1p33s2).[10] We also see it in the appendix to the opening part of the
Ethics, where he claims that providentialism, or the view that "God
himself directs all things to some certain end" (1app; G II, 78) is
the root of prejudices and "a great obstacle to men's understanding
the connection of things" (G II, 77). As Spinoza memorably puts
it in the same appendix, those who seek to explain things through
divine providence take shelter in "the sanctuary of ignorance" (G
II, 81). He proceeds to rail against those who conceive of God as
a kind of benevolent legislator or king elsewhere in the *Ethics* and
in his *Theological-Political Treatise*, where, in a familiar fashion, he
criticizes those who "imagine powers numerically distinct from
one another, the power of God and the power of natural things
[…]. But what do they understand by these two powers, and by
God and nature? They don't know, of course, except that they
imagine God's power as the rule of a certain royal majesty" (TTP
6.2; G III, 81).[11] The view of God as a kind of divine legislator who
metes out punishments and who promises transcendental rewards
serves as an obstacle to science or knowledge and keeps people in
a slavish, fearful condition, perpetually anxious about the afterlife.
If this were not bad enough, traditional philosophical theology
lends itself to political strife since it leaves room for considerable
interpretative dispute over what counts as revelation and divine
law. Recognizing this, Spinoza undertook a work, the TTP, that
sought to reconceptualize what true religion and faith consist
in, a work that would protect society from the abuses of zealous
theologians and clerics and would liberate individuals from fear
and hatred.

3.3 The main objectives of the
Theological-Political Treatise

In a 1665 letter to Henry Oldenburg, then Secretary of the Royal Society, Spinoza describes the three things that motivated him to begin composing what would become the *Theological-Political Treatise*:

1 the prejudices of the theologians; for I know that they are the greatest obstacle to men's being able to apply their minds to philosophy; so I am busy exposing them and removing them from the minds of the more prudent;

2 the opinion the common people have of me; they never stop accusing me of atheism, and I am forced to rebut this accusation as well as I can; and

3 the freedom of philosophizing and saying what we think, which I want to defend in every way; here the preachers suppress it as much as they can with their excessive authority and aggressiveness. (Ep. 30)

The second reason provides further evidence that Spinoza earnestly thought of himself not as an antireligious thinker but as a kind of religious reformer. However, he was clearly naive to think that others would have received him in the way that he conceived of himself. Rather than silencing the charge of atheism, the publication of the TTP only stimulated more virulent accusations as soon as it was discovered that Spinoza was indeed the author of this anonymously published work, which did not take long.

The first and the third reasons are what really animate and give structure to the work. The former is concerned with superstition, the latter with persecution. As Spinoza sees it, these two maladies share a common root: a politically powerful clergy. Spinoza thus organizes the TTP around protecting the state from the abuses of the clergy. We will later consider more directly the ways the work seeks to protect against religious persecution.[12] Here, though, we will look at the first substantial layer of his anticlerical project, namely, his attempt to limit the scope of theological concern. Specifically, he advances a very minimal conception of faith that is not tied to any particular creed or dogma and does not require philosophical insight or hermeneutic expertise. At one point, he calls the task of separating faith from philosophy – which we will refer to as the

Separation Thesis – the "main purpose of this whole work" (TTP 14.5; G III, 174). The first fifteen chapters of the TTP can be seen as a systemic argument for the Separation Thesis. In a moment, we will turn to consider the stages of this argument. First, though, it will be helpful to situate the work in its historical context so that we can better understand the exigencies that led to its composition.

3.4 The context of the *Theological-Political Treatise*

In the subtitle of the work, Spinoza claims that he will show "that the republic can grant freedom of philosophizing without harming its peace or piety, and cannot deny it without destroying its peace and piety." Spinoza is intervening here in the protracted struggle over Dutch identity that shaped much of the political debate in the United Provinces after it established independence from Spain. On the one hand, there were those who thought that, having fought for their own freedom from the oppressive and intolerant Spanish Hapsburgs, the Dutch Republic was a commonwealth founded on the principle of confessional freedom. Their vision was, in some respects, the law. The Dutch Republic took a relatively permissive approach to religious practice, allowing Lutherans, Mennonites, Anabaptists, Collegiants, Quakers, and even Jews and Catholics to practice their faiths, even if it initially denied full citizenship rights to the latter two groups. And the freedom of religious practice in at least some of the provinces was protected by Article XIII of the Union of Utrecht (1579), one of the foundational documents of the republic. By praising Dutch freedom, Spinoza is lending his weight to the tolerationist model of national identity.

However, there were also those who viewed the nascent republic as an unreconstructed Calvinist state, regarding the Dutch revolt as an essentially Calvinist uprising against a Catholic oppressor. Those who saw the Dutch Republic as a fundamentally Calvinist state sought for the Reformed Church to have a greater influence over civic life. The theocratic pretensions of the Calvinists are expressed by Article XXXVI of the Belgic Confession, which codified the main doctrines of the faith: "[T]he government's task is not limited to caring for and watching over the public domain but extends also to upholding the sacred ministry, with a view to removing and destroying all idolatry and false worship of the Antichrist."[13] Civic authorities are positioned to do God's work on earth, including punishing heretics. Consequently, on this vision, laws against blasphemy and heresy more generally were an essential, not an aberrant, part of a Calvinist state.

The struggle between tolerationists and Calvinist hardliners over national identity, confessional freedom, and the relationship between church and state persisted throughout the seventeenth century, taking a number of different forms. The conflict between the Remonstrants and the Counter-Remonstrants in the early decades of the century set the terms for much of the subsequent dispute. The Remonstrants were followers of Jacobus Arminius (hence their other designation, "Arminians") who articulated the ways in which they deviated from orthodox Calvinism in a formal "Remonstrance" in 1610. One of their core tenets was that faith is expressed in the conscience of the individual and is therefore not subject to the coercive power of the state. The Remonstrants were opposed by the conservative Gomarists (followers of Franciscus Gomarus), or Counter-Remonstrants. This dispute raged for a little over a decade, before a national ecclesiastical council, the Synod of Dort, convened in 1618 to define more precisely the parameters of public faith. The fallout from the Synod was disastrous for the Arminians. The Synod rejected the grounds of remonstrance, and Arminians throughout the country were purged from town councils and universities.[14]

This episode cast a long shadow over Dutch political life. The middle of the century witnessed an aftershock that centered on university life. Once again, two theologians were at the heart of the debate: Johannes Cocceius, a liberal theology professor at Leiden, and Gisbertus Voetius, dean of the University of Utrecht. Disputes between Cocceians and Voetians began over abstruse theological matters but expanded into more general disagreements about the relationships between religion, natural philosophy, and politics. The Voetians led the assault on the Cartesian philosophy being taught in the universities. Spinoza's philosophy was criticized by *both* the Voetians and the Cocceian-Cartesians, but it was the Voetians who posed the greatest threat to Spinoza and his circle since they were bent on punishing freethinkers and reining in philosophers, invoking theology to justify the expansion of blasphemy laws.

Spinoza was of course personally familiar with intolerance. In addition to being cast out of the Jewish community by the Amsterdam rabbinate, Spinoza saw his friend Lodewijk Meyer's *Philosophia S. Scripturae Interpres* viciously condemned upon its publication in 1666 and their mutual friend Adriaan Koerbagh tried and sentenced for blasphemy for publishing his libertine

ideas in two treatises in 1668. Koerbagh ridiculed a number of
traditional religious doctrines and practices, while advancing his
own shocking views, among which were: Jesus is not divine; God
is identical with nature; everything is necessitated by the laws of
nature (the laws of God); and miracles are impossible. These are
all positions that Spinoza consistently endorsed. However, while
Spinoza was famously cautious, Koerbagh was not, publishing
the works in Dutch – and thereby making them accessible to the
general literate public – under his own name. During his subsequent imprisonment under squalid conditions Koerbagh became
ill, and he died soon thereafter in 1669.

3.5 The argument for the Separation Thesis[15]

The Separation Thesis is, at its core, a repudiation of the view
that Scripture gives us knowledge of God, his attributes, and the
operations of nature. The establishment of this thesis is the main
aim of the first fifteen chapters of the work. We may divide the
structure of the argument into five discrete dialectical moves: (1)
adopt a minimal interpretative method (preface); (2) challenge
the view of Scripture as the source of knowledge of God (chapters
1–6); (3) advance a naturalistic interpretative method (chapter 7);
(4) decisively reject the view that Scripture is a work of divinely
revealed metaphysics (chapters 8–12); (5) articulate a stripped-
down conception of faith and the function of Scripture (chapters
13–15). We will briefly consider these stages in turn.

Stage one: adopt a minimal method (preface)

The religious disputes that shook the Dutch Republic in the seventeenth century turned on metaphysical interpretations of Scripture.
Spinoza challenges a methodological assumption on which these
interpretations depend, namely, that the claims of the Bible must
be true on account of the text's divine origin. To assume without
further examination that this text is the unvarnished word of God
is to commit a form of idolatry, which Spinoza rails against, both in
the preface, where he criticizes superstitious common people who
"worship the books of Scripture rather than the Word of God itself"
(TTP preface; G III, 10), and in chapter 12, where he accuses those
who "worship likenesses and images, i.e. paper and ink, in place of

the Word of God" (TTP 12.5; G III, 159) of converting religion into superstition.

In the preface to the TTP, Spinoza clearly delineates the methodological assumption that he opposes:

> [Most] presuppose, as a foundation for understanding Scripture and unearthing its true meaning, that it is everywhere true and divine. So what we ought to establish by understanding Scripture, and subjecting it to a strict examination, and what we would be far better taught by Scripture itself, which needs no human inventions, they maintain at the outset as a rule for the interpretation of Scripture. (G III, 9)

Spinoza resolves to eschew such idolatry and "examine Scripture afresh, with an unprejudiced and free spirit, to affirm nothing about it, and to admit nothing as its teaching, which it did not very clearly teach me" (TTP preface; G III, 9).

Of course, Spinoza could not open the work by assuming that Scripture is just a text like any other without alienating his readership. Instead, he proposes merely that we read Scripture with an "unprejudiced and free spirit" so as to discover, rather than merely assume *ex ante*, whether the text supplies genuine knowledge about God and the universe. Spinoza's suggestion in the next stage is that it does not.

Stage two: critique of revelation (chapters 1–6)

The first six chapters of the work provide a critique of revelation. Spinoza opens the work with an analysis of prophets and prophecy, noting that "prophecy is inferior to natural knowledge" since the former depends on the latter to certify its claims (TTP 2.5; G III, 30). Prophetic knowledge is rooted in the imagination, which Spinoza presents as the lowest form of cognition in the *Ethics* (2p40s2).[16] He claims that prophecies reveal more about the temperament of the prophet than they do about Nature or God's will (TTP 2.12; G III, 32).[17] The key point is that the declarations of prophets should thus not be taken as the source of metaphysical insight. Still, prophets were good moral models, having minds "inclined only to the right and the good" (TTP 2.10; G III, 31). This is a bracing opening. Spinoza is already suggesting that Scripture does not reveal deep truths about God or Nature but, rather, aims only at moral instruction.

Spinoza extends his critique of revelation in chapters 3–6, where he confronts the status of Jewish election, Mosaic Law, divine providence, divine law, and miracles. In these chapters, he presents compact statements of central features of his philosophical theology that seem to conflict with how Scripture is ordinarily understood. For instance, he maintains that God acts from a fixed and immutable nature (TTP 4.37, 6.25; G III, 65, 86) and that he does not love one part of creation more than the rest (TTP 3.12; G III, 46–7). To the extent that Scripture contradicts these tenets, it is the source of metaphysical confusion.

His analysis of miracles brings us back to his critique of traditional philosophical theology. He lambasts the ignorant for conceiving of God as a kind of supreme potentate and for supposing that God's work is most evident when things are least understood. Instead, he reaffirms that "God's intellect is not distinguished from his will" (TTP 6.8; G III, 82), that God acts according to fixed and eternal laws, and that "if someone were to maintain that God does something contrary to the laws of nature, he would be compelled to maintain at the same time also that God acts in a way contrary to his own nature" (TTP 6.9; G III, 83). In short, there are no genuine miracles or violations of the laws of nature. And apparent miracles reveal nothing but the ignorance of the perceiver, supplying no knowledge about the essence or existence of God. On the contrary, the more we understand things through the laws of nature, the better we know God's will. Where Scripture seems to present miraculous events and to portray these violations of the laws of nature as the work of God, it advances patently false views.

Rather than baldly concluding that Scripture supplies us with nothing but bad philosophy, Spinoza proceeds to argue that much of what looks like confused metaphysics can be attributed to the cramped perspectives of the characters. Adam conceives of God as a kind of supreme legislator who issues violable edicts "because of a defect in his knowledge" (TTP 4.27; G III, 63). The same holds for the Israelites, who view God confusedly as one who issued edicts for their special benefit (TTP 4.27; G III, 63). And when Scripture actually relays the views of those who are held to be wise, like Solomon and Christ, we find that their ideas agree with reason. From Solomon, for instance, we learn that everything follows from the laws of nature (TTP 6.67–8; G III, 95) and that true happiness lies in knowledge and virtue (TTP 4; G III, 66–8). Christ is presented as having grasped God's laws adequately as eternal truths rather than as commands (TTP 4; G III, 64–5).

Moreover, naturalistic explanations are available to account for apparent violations of metaphysical principles. Jewish election can and should be understood as the civic flourishing of a stubborn, slavish people that is explicable in terms of the laws of social coordination (TTP 5.16–18; G III, 73). What is reported as miraculous from one perspective is often recounted elsewhere with reference to the natural causes (TTP 6.45; G III, 90). And finally, according to Spinoza, some of what look like claims of divine interventions in the operations of nature appear that way only because we lack knowledge of Hebrew figures of speech (TTP 6.59–63; G III, 93–4). Based on such considerations, Spinoza concludes that "you will find almost nothing in Scripture which can be demonstrated to be contrary to the light of nature" (TTP 6.64; G III, 94).

We should not infer from this that Spinoza thinks that Scripture is philosophically insightful. At its core, Scripture is a collection of narratives written for ordinary people, and the thrust of Scripture is non-philosophical – it presents, at least on the surface, a confused view of God, suited to unrefined minds.

Stage three: the interpretative method (chapter 7)

Having punctured the ideal of Scripture as an unerring guide to metaphysical truths, Spinoza may now explicate his full interpretative method in TTP 7. The central proposal of this chapter is that we approach Scripture in a way that is consistent with the interpretation of nature (TTP 7.6–8; G III, 98). This requires that we inquire into the conditions of its composition – the "life, character, and concerns of the author" (TTP 7.23; G III, 102) – and that we gain familiarity with the language in which the text was written (TTP 7.44; G III, 106). Moreover, in order to identify its central claims, we must proceed in our study of Scripture from that which is "universal and common to the whole" to those things that are less universal (TTP 7.27–9; G III, 102–3). Following this naturalistic method enables Spinoza to complete his case against Scripture as metaphysics and defend the separation of faith from philosophy.

It is worth pausing for a moment to take note of what is distinctive about Spinoza's method for interpreting Scripture. As he sees it, most readers of Scripture just assume from the authority of the Bible without critical examination – which, again, he regards as a kind of idolatry. Scriptural idolaters fall into two camps. One camp, which Spinoza dubs the "dogmatists" (TTP 15), assumes that

Scripture is an unerring source of *rational* metaphysical knowledge. According to this group – which includes Moses Maimonides and Spinoza's friend Lodewijk Meyer – the claims of Scripture must be adapted to accord with reason. While the dogmatists are right to regard reason as the ultimate arbiter of metaphysical knowledge, they are wrong to treat the Bible as if it were a work of philosophy (TTP 15; G III, 113–16). To start from the assumption that this particular text is unfailingly rational is to abdicate reason, which demands that the credibility of a text be established through its content, and not brutely assumed.

The second form of Scriptural idolatry assumes that Scripture is an unerring source of metaphysical knowledge while denying that reason is the only standard for metaphysical knowledge. This group, whom Spinoza calls the "skeptics," make reason subservient to faith, claiming that when philosophy and Scripture conflict, it is Scripture to which we must defer. Spinoza agrees with the skeptics that there can be genuine incompatibility between what Scripture and reason maintain, but he denounces the way that they "want to make reason, [God's] greatest gift, a divine light, subordinate to dead letters – which men's wicked conduct could have corrupted" (TTP 15.10; G III, 182). This is the height of epistemic absurdity. Dogmatists and skeptics alike fail to read Scripture critically because they are antecedently committed to its authority as a revealed, metaphysical text. By contrast, Spinoza thinks that a scientific examination of the Bible shows that it is a fallible, human document, whose value is primarily moral.

Stage four: the full rejection of Scripture as metaphysics (chapters 8–12)

In the subsequent cluster of chapters, Spinoza deploys the naturalistic method, challenging a host of traditional claims about Scripture and its authorship. He maintains here that Scripture is an artifact through and through, a potpourri of fables assembled to suit the interests of its editors. Spinoza denies that Moses was the sole author of the Pentateuch, questions the authorship of Joshua, Judges, Ruth, and Samuel, and claims that the canonical books of the Old Testament were fixed by a council of fallible Pharisees (TTP 10.43–4; G III, 150).

Having argued that Scripture is a patchwork and utterly human document, Spinoza pivots to ward off the accusation that this renders Scripture profane. He maintains, first, that the most general teachings of Scripture – simple truths about God (that he exists, is omnipotent, etc.) and the core teachings of morality – are consistent with reason and "inscribed by divine agency in men's hearts, i.e., in the human mind" (TTP 12.2; G III, 158). Moreover, he argues that "nothing is sacred or profane or impure in itself, outside the mind, but only in relation to the mind" (TTP 12.12; G III, 160). The sanctity or profanity of a text is determined by its effects on the reader. Just as words acquire meaning from their usage, the significance of full texts depends on their function. A text is sacred only insofar as it moves people to devotion and adherence to God's word. The implication is clear: those who would turn Scripture into a superstitious doctrine and promote hatred and conflict are the real heretics, as they render the text profane. Spinoza aims to restore Scripture's sacred status by distilling Scripture to its core moral teachings.

Stage five: faith and the Separation Thesis (chapters 13–15)

Chapters 13–15 complete the case for the Separation Thesis. When we look to Scripture to find the prevalent teachings that operate as its "universal principles," we discover that the central teachings exhort obedience to God and love of one's neighbor – the latter being the whole of the law.[18] This leads Spinoza to embrace a functional conception of the faith as that set of beliefs – which may vary from individual to individual – that conduce to justice and charity. While there is some thin content to faith in the sense that there are doctrines of the universal faith that one must acknowledge in order to exhibit obedience to God, these dogmas are left deliberately indeterminate, so that they may be accommodated to suit the mind of the individual (TTP 14.32; G III, 178). Faith does not require that one's beliefs have any specific, robust content. It requires commitment to certain very general principles without which justice and charity are not possible. The crucial point here is that Scripture does not demand that one form a true understanding of God. It merely requires commitment to whatever set of ideas encourage justice and charity (TTP 13.24; G III, 171).

We can now appreciate the full force of Spinoza's Separation Thesis. Despite the language of separation, faith does really not have its own jurisdiction since philosophy confirms and grounds the very moral principles that are central to faith. If faith has a unique social role, it is as a source of moral instruction for those who are incapable of reason. Faith and reason are only partially separate and certainly not equal.

The Separation Thesis diminishes the scope over which a clergy could preside. Because Scripture does not require belief in any specific creeds, and because the moral message of the Bible is apparent on its face, there is no need for an interpretative vanguard to decipher the "true" message of Scripture. Instead of acting as interpreters of divine mysteries, the role of the clergy is restricted to promoting the Bible's message of justice and charity.

3.6 True religion

After completing the case for the Separation Thesis, Spinoza observes: "How salutary this doctrine is, how necessary in the republic, if people are to live peacefully and harmoniously, how many, and how great, are the causes of disturbance and wickedness it prevents" (TTP 14.34; G III, 179). A proper understanding of faith contributes to civic health in two ways. First, it encourages a generally tolerant approach to religious belief. Second, it paves the way for a political understanding of piety that might contribute to social cohesion. Let us briefly consider each of these points.

Spinoza's content-neutral conception of faith encourages a laissez-faire approach to religious belief, according to which each person may understand biblical teachings in whatever way best encourages her commitment to justice and charity (TTP 14.3; G III, 173). Because human belief systems are so diverse that "what moves one person to religion moves another to laughter" (TTP preface; G III, 11) and because at its core faith exhorts only that we worship God and love our neighbor, we ought to grant individuals full interpretative latitude consistent with this conception of faith. This promotes personal toleration, encouraging individuals to check the natural assumption that others ought to believe whatever one herself believes. And when Spinoza asserts that "[t]he worship of God and obedience to him consist only in justice and loving-kindness, *or* in love towards one's neighbor" (TTP 14.27; G III, 177) is one of the seven dogmas of universal faith that all civil subjects must accept, he is effectively promoting a policy of toleration, such that one does not take one's own specific religious beliefs as prescriptive for all of humanity.[19]

The other chief salutary function of public religion lies in its capacity to boost national solidarity. We see this in Spinoza's analysis of universal religion (TTP 14, TP 8/46–8), which is a kind of antidote to exclusivist religions. The universal religion aims at once to break the harmful effects of exceptionalism while encouraging a degree of social cohesion. In addition to the view that faith consists only in love of one's neighbor, the other six doctrines assert that God exists, is unique, omniscient, and omnipotent; that those who obey him through loving their neighbor are saved; and that God pardons repentant sinners. While Spinoza claims that none of these doctrines is controversial among honest men (TTP 14.22; G III, 177), scholars have wondered whether Spinoza himself could endorse any version of the last two claims. However, given the latitude he accords the individual to construe these doctrines – such that "salvation" (*salus*) could be understood as a kind of flourishing and God's forgiveness could be taken to mean simply that no one is irrevocably condemned to a life of suffering and that those who are moved to improve their character may reap the rewards therefrom – there is reason to suppose that even Spinoza could accept them. While the seven "doctrines of the universal faith" may be quite thin, they provide some sort of common ground to which all citizens may appeal, rather than fixating on doctrinal difference.

There is a precarious balance here. Civil religion must be thin enough to accommodate a wide range of beliefs, while being thick enough to promote a sense of cohesion. While one might reasonably doubt whether the norms of tolerance and solidarity can be jointly satisfied, this is Spinoza's aim. A proper conception of faith – with its public and private dimensions – can mitigate the place of pride and envy in civil life, replacing superstition, parochialism, and hatred with tolerance and, to a degree, solidarity.

Further reading

Donagan, Alan. 1988. *Spinoza*. Chicago: University of Chicago Press, ch. 2.

Huenemann, Charlie. 2014. *Spinoza's Radical Theology: The Metaphysics of the Infinite*. London: Routledge.

James, Susan. 2012. *Spinoza on Philosophy, Religion, and Politics: The Theologico-Political Treatise*. Oxford: Oxford University Press, chs 1–9.

Nadler, Steven. 2011. *A Book Forged in Hell: Spinoza's Scandalous Treatise and the Birth of the Secular Age*. Princeton: Princeton University Press.

Preus, J. Samuel. 2001. *Spinoza and the Irrelevance of Biblical Authority*. Cambridge: Cambridge University Press.

4

Knowledge and the Human Mind

Most people today tend to think that knowledge starts with the senses. There are strong philosophical roots for this belief. During Spinoza's era, the Aristotelians were the most prominent promoters of this line of thought: after all, their basic epistemological dictum is that "nothing is in the intellect that was not first in the senses." Another major trend, arguably launched by Descartes, is that epistemology has come to revolve around the finite human subject. Spinoza's theory of knowledge goes decidedly against both empiricism and human-centered epistemology: he does not think that we should start with sense experience of the individual subject and then expand out. This also makes it a rather difficult theory for us to understand. However, his approach offers not only a powerful alternative view of knowledge but also an attractive view of the mind–body relation that avoids some of the thorniest problems associated with Cartesian dualism. His view of mind also includes a prescient and economical account of belief that involves the rejection of faculty theories, which fell into disrepute during the early modern era.

4.1 Ontology of cognition

We have seen that, for Spinoza, there is only one substance, God or Nature, and that finite things, like us, are just modifications of this substance. Understandably but still strikingly enough, Spinoza's basic ontology influences how he thinks about epistemological

matters. Spinoza believes that knowledge begins with an understanding of God or Nature, and that it is only after proper
consideration of the divine nature that we can come to understand
where we fit into the picture. In the very informative scholium to
2p10, Spinoza takes aim at his Cartesian and Aristotelian predecessors for failing to follow the proper order of philosophizing:

> Everyone, of course, must concede that nothing can either be or be
> conceived without God. For all confess that God is the only cause of
> all things, both of their essence and of their existence. I.e., God is not
> only the cause of the coming to be of things, as they say, but also of
> their being.
>
> But in the meantime many say that anything without which a
> thing can neither be nor be conceived pertains to the nature of the
> thing. And so they believe either that the nature of God pertains
> to the essence of created things, or that created things can be or be
> conceived without God – or what is more certain, they are not suffi-
> ciently consistent.
>
> The cause of this, I believe, was that *they did not observe the [proper]
> order of philosophizing*. For *they believed that the divine nature, which
> they should have contemplated before all else* (because it is prior both
> in knowledge and in nature) is last in the order of knowledge, and
> that the things that are called objects of the senses are prior to all.
> That is why, when they contemplated natural things, they thought of
> nothing less than they did of the divine nature; and when afterwards
> they directed their minds to contemplating the divine nature, they
> could think of nothing less than of their first fictions, on which they
> had built the knowledge of natural things, because these could not
> assist knowledge of the divine nature. So it is no wonder that they
> have generally contradicted themselves. (2p10s, emphases added)

The passage is built on the traditional distinction between the order
of knowledge (*ordo cognoscendi*) and the order of being (*ordo essendi*).
Even though the vast majority of Spinoza's predecessors were
unafraid to espouse large-scale metaphysical systems, in the order
of knowledge ideas of particular things (such as horses and tables)
were considered the starting points from which our cognition
can then ascend to more general things, such as animality and
rationality, the teleological cosmic order of things, and ultimately
God (who is first in the order of being). For instance, although
Descartes is keen to emphasize the role of God for our cognition,
it is still true that the beginning of the *Meditations* is decidedly
centered on the cognition of the finite human individual, as most
famously expressed by the *cogito* thesis. Against this, Spinoza

insists that the order of knowledge must match the order of being; this view has been characterized as the *top-down model*. Already in the early *Treatise on the Emendation of the Intellect*, Spinoza goes decidedly against human subject-centered epistemology, making the following rather startling declarations:

> [S]ince it is clear through itself that the mind understands itself the better, the more it understands of Nature, it is evident, from that that this part of the method will be more perfect as the mind understands more things, and will be most perfect when the mind attends to, *or* reflects on, knowledge of the most perfect being. (TIE, §39)

> When we came to know this method, we saw [...] that it will be most perfect when we have the idea of the most perfect being. So in the beginning we must take the greatest care that we arrive at knowledge of such a being as quickly as possible. (TIE, §49)

In other words, according to both the young and mature Spinoza, adequate cognition *begins with* the idea of "the most perfect being" or "divine nature" and then *descends* to ontologically and, correspondingly, epistemologically posterior things, from God's attributes to infinite modes to finite modes,[1] such as Bengal cats, Birmans, and British Shorthairs.

Given Spinoza's monism and the philosophical theology that it entails, it is not surprising that the second part of the *Ethics*, dedicated to epistemological issues, begins precisely with God's thought and of all those things that are its objects. Accordingly, in 2p3–p6 Spinoza emphasizes that God as a thinking thing has ideas of all things no matter under which attribute they fall.[2] This thesis builds on the view that since God produces everything he understands (1p16), the causal and epistemic realms fall into line: there could never be anything outside the immanent God that could give rise to disagreement between God's intellect and things produced by God. This is certainly one of the main reasons why Spinoza is convinced that reality is, in itself, thoroughly intelligible – although that conviction no doubt has other sources as well, such as the Galileo-Cartesian idea of extended nature as geometrically structured, and hence deep down as intelligible as mathematics.

What is the ontological status of the human mind in this framework? True to his top-down approach, Spinoza explains:

> [T]he human mind is a part of the infinite intellect of God. Therefore, when we say that the human mind perceives this or that, we are

saying nothing but that God, not insofar as he is infinite, but insofar as he is explained through the nature of the human mind, or insofar as he constitutes the essence of the human mind, has this or that idea[.] (2p11c)

All this is quite consistent with the thesis that in a monistic system, the whole – God or Nature – is ontologically prior to everything else, including human minds. They are thus not ontologically independent substances but modifications of God or Nature and as such parts of the infinite intellect of God. So, when, for instance, Mary sees a cat in front of her, what happens, according to Spinoza, is that God insofar as it is modified in the manner that *is* Mary's mind, perceives the cat, another finite modification of God.

Consistency aside, Spinoza's subversive epistemological strategy is bound to take us by surprise – which is something Spinoza admits. Right after the corollary he inserts the following scholium: "Here, no doubt, my readers will come to a halt, and think of many things which will give them pause. For this reason I ask them to continue on with me slowly, step by step, and to make no judgment on these matters until they have read through them all" (2p11s).

Obviously, Spinoza is convinced that once the reader has fully appreciated the big picture, she will be prepared to accept the God-driven epistemology as well. Still, this does not remove the fact that epistemology might be the most difficult aspect of Spinoza's system to accept, regardless of how enthusiastic one may be of his naturalistic identification of God and Nature. But while the epistemological approach may be counterintuitive for many, still it yields a view of the relationship between mind and body, the main features of which many regard as quite compelling.

4.2 Mind–body relation

Perhaps the most widely known, and almost as widely denounced, feature of Cartesian rationalism is its strict distinction between mind and body. Traditionally, substancehood was seen to have two aspects: a substance must be, first, ontologically independent and, second, the bearer of other, ontologically dependent entities, usually called properties, qualities, or accidents. As we have seen,[3] Descartes is willing to loosen the most literal requirement of substancehood – which God alone fulfills – and treat mind and body as substances because they need "only the concurrence of

God in order to exist" (*Principles* I.52; CSM I, 210). But he is not willing to let go of the doctrine that mind and body are *really distinct* substances, which "we can clearly and distinctly understand" (*Principles* I.60; CSM I, 213) apart from each other. He continues: "Similarly, from the mere fact that each of us understands himself to be a thinking thing and is capable, in thought, of excluding from himself every other substance, whether thinking or extended, it is certain that each of us, regarded in this way, is really distinct from every other thinking substance and from every corporeal substance" (*Principles* I.60; CSM I, 213).

Similarly and even more famously, Descartes of the Second Meditation identifies himself with thinking:

> I am, then, in the strict sense only a thing that thinks; that is, I am a mind, or intelligence, or intellect, or reason – words whose meaning I have been ignorant of until now. But for all that I am a thing which is real and which truly exists. But what kind of a thing? As I have just said – a thinking thing. (CSM II, 18)[4]

And although he is considerably more circumspect concerning the status of the bodily substance, Descartes ends up by declaring, in the Sixth Meditation, that "[t]here is nothing that my own nature teaches me more vividly than that I have a body" (CSM II, 56).[5]

Understandably enough, Cartesian mind–body dualism puzzled his readers from early on. If mind and body are really distinct substances, with principal attributes having *nothing* in common, exactly how is interaction between mind and body possible? Descartes was rather elusive about this conundrum. Still, after Princess Elisabeth of Bohemia had pressed the issue in the 1643 correspondence, he had no choice but to confront the issue. Descartes begins by stating that he endorses two tenets concerning the human mind: "The first is that it thinks, the second is that, being united to the body, it can act and be acted upon along with it" (CSMK, 218). He rightly admits that "[a]bout the second I have said hardly anything," for the somewhat striking reason that "my principal aim was to prove the distinction between the soul and the body, and to this end only the first was useful, and *the second might have been harmful*" (CSMK, 218, emphasis added). By Elisabeth's request, however, Descartes elaborates on his understanding of substantial union of mind and body:

> First I consider that there are in us certain *primitive notions* which are as it were the patterns on the basis of which we form all our other

conceptions. There are very few such notions. First, there are the most general – those of being, number, duration, etc. – which apply to everything we can conceive. Then, as regards body in particular, we have only the notion of extension, which entails the notions of shape and motion; and as regards the soul on its own, we have only the notion of thought, which includes the perceptions of the intellect and the inclinations of the will. Lastly, *as regards the soul and the body together, we have only the notion of their union, on which depends our notion of the soul's power to move the body, and the body's power to act on the soul and cause its sensations and passions.* (CSMK, 218, emphases added)

He continues by emphasizing that these primitive notions should be carefully kept apart. This certainly sounds like a reasonable piece of advice but tells us little about the notion of the mind–body union. Accordingly, Elisabeth continues to press the issue further. In response, Descartes advances what might be broadly characterized as a *phenomenological* approach.[6] While "[t]he soul is conceived only by the pure intellect" and the body can "likewise be known by the intellect alone, but much better by the intellect aided by the imagination," the mind–body union is *"known only obscurely by the intellect alone or even by the intellect aided by the imagination, but it is known very clearly by the senses.* That is why *people who never philosophize* and use only their senses have no doubt that the soul moves the body and that the body acts on the soul" (CSMK, 227, emphases added). So, surprisingly for a thinker traditionally regarded as one of the great rationalists of the modern era, attempting to grasp the mind–body union by using one's intellect is not the way to proceed; rather, "it is the ordinary course of life and conversation, and abstention from meditation and from the study of the things which exercise the imagination, that teaches us how to conceive the union of the soul and the body" (CSMK, 227). Indeed, "[e]veryone feels that he is a single person with both body and thought so related by nature that the thought can move the body and feel the things which happen to it" (CSMK, 228).

One way to understand what Descartes is claiming here is to see him as recommending abstaining from philosophy so as to discover that in our ordinary existence we have an intelligible enough notion of mind–body interaction[7]; adopting a therapeutic rather than argumentative approach helps us to realize that unreflective daily life is enough to grasp the nature of mind–body union. However, one might wonder whether his maneuvers amount to much more than a description of the problem.[8] Descartes has been widely considered to have ended up with a deeply problematic dualist conception of human beings, a conception whose shortcomings Spinoza is convinced his monistic approach does not have. Moreover, and in keeping with his rationalist modus operandi, Spinoza presents his view of the mind–body relationship in a tightly argued package designed to be primarily accessible precisely to the intellect.[9]

To understand Spinoza's line of thought, we must recall his top-down approach in epistemology since his solution to the mind–body relationship is based on that approach. We will present Spinoza's account in three steps. First, he does his best to argue that finite things – human minds and bodies included – are produced by their respective attributes alone. We have already encountered what has come to be termed the conceptual barrier between the attributes[10]; in the beginning of the second part of the *Ethics*, Spinoza emphasizes that there is a causal barrier as well: "The modes of each attribute have God for their cause only insofar as he is considered under the attribute of which they are modes, and not insofar as he is considered under any other attribute" (2p6). The crucial proof reads:

> For each attribute is conceived through itself without any other (by 1p10). So the modes of each attribute involve the concept of their own attribute, but not of another one; and so (by 1a4) they have God for their cause only insofar as he is considered under the attribute of which they are modes, and not insofar as he is considered under any other. (2p6d)

In other words, Spinoza argues that since modifications (like all effects) must be conceived through their causes, they must be conceived through their *own* attributes. The line of reasoning seems to be as follows. Should any modification m of the attribute E be conceivable through another attribute T,[11] it would follow that m would *not* be conceived through E alone (but also through T). And this, of course, would violate the epistemologically self-sufficient status of an attribute (or, to put it otherwise, would infringe the conceptual barrier). As a consequence, the human mind and body must be conceived through – and given the coextensiveness of conception and causation – *and caused by* their respective attributes, thought and extension, *alone*.[12] The first step of Spinoza's argument is thus deeply embedded within his philosophical system.

The second step is formed by the proposition as renowned as it is difficult: "The order and connection of ideas is the same as the order and connection of things" (2p7). The demonstration of this pivotal proposition, usually taken as the statement of what is called *"parallelism,"* is frustratingly brief: "This is clear from 1a4. For the idea of each thing caused depends on the knowledge of the cause of which it is the effect." However, keeping in mind the previous proposition and its demonstration, perhaps Spinoza's extremely compressed manner of expression is not as abstruse as has been thought. The fact that the demonstration of 2p6 is also based on 1a4 offers, we believe, a lead: in 2p7d, Spinoza is referring to his view of the way in which cognition and causation fall in line. In fact, he had just reminded us that

> the formal being of things which are not modes of thinking does not follow from the divine nature because [God] has first known the things; rather *the objects of ideas follow and are inferred from their attributes* in the same way and by the same necessity as that with which we have shown ideas to follow from the attribute of thought. (2p6c, emphasis added)

As we see it, this corollary expresses relatively clearly the rationale behind 2p7. All things follow from their attributes, and because, as we have seen, God forms modes of thought (i.e., ideas) of (and only of) everything it causes, the order and connection of ideas cannot but mirror the order and connection of things. Spinoza confirms this in 2p7c. In this basic sense, all things are objects of God's ideas.

The final step is taken immediately after the second, and it consists of what is, in essence, Spinoza's view of the mind–body union. Consistently enough, it proceeds in the top-down fashion:

> [W]e must recall here what we showed [...], viz. that whatever can be perceived by an infinite intellect as constituting an essence of substance *pertains to one substance only*, and consequently that *the thinking substance and the extended substance are one and the same substance, which is now comprehended under this attribute, now under that. So also a mode of extension and the idea of that mode are one and the same thing, but expressed in two ways.* [...] For example, a circle existing in nature and the idea of the existing circle, which is also in God, are one and the same thing, which is explained through different attributes. (2p7s, emphases added)[13]

In other words, Spinoza claims that monism and necessitarianism coupled with conceptual dualism (or pluralism) yields the result that any object and the idea of that object are "one and the same thing, but expressed in two ways." This of course cannot but apply to human beings: "The object of the idea constituting the human mind is the body, *or* a certain mode of extension which actually exists, and nothing else" (2p13).

The demonstration certainly has its twists and turns, but its message is relatively clear: our mind must be about something – that is, it must have an object. Given that we only know ideas and bodies (2a5), the only thing that could be the object of our mind is a body, namely the body that we immediately feel (2a4). And so, at long last, Spinoza reaches, as the corollary of this proposition, the key statement: "From this it follows that man consists of a mind and a body, and that the human body exists, as we are aware of it" (2p13c). Thus, for Spinoza, mind–body union is a *consequence* of his divine-laden epistemology, and the human body is *the object of* the human mind. Spinoza reveals how pleased he is with the way in which his account avoids the Cartesian troubles, writing: "From these [propositions] we understand not only that the human mind is united to the body, but also what should be understood by the union of mind and body" (2p13s).[14] Whatever concerns one might have about Spinoza's account of the mind–body union, at least it is not vulnerable to the problems plaguing (Cartesian) interactionism, since it is not a form of interactionism in the first place.[15] We will later discuss the most important facets and ramifications of Spinoza's account[16]; for the present purposes it suffices to note that, on Spinoza's account, mind and body are "one and the same thing" only "expressed in two ways" (2p7d). The Spinozistic framework thus accounts for the unity of the human mind and body without denying the conceptual distinction between these two aspects of our being. This position has been praised as an early modern precursor of nowadays common identity theories – and even regarded as something that anticipates the so-called "embodied mind" research programs.[17]

4.3 Sense perception and inadequate knowledge

We can now turn to the other major strand in Spinoza's episte-mology, namely its anti-empiricism. Already in 1663, in a letter to Meyer, he expresses his low regard for sense experience somewhat informally:

> [S]ince there are many things which we cannot at all grasp by the imagination [i.e., by sense experience], but only by the intellect (such

as substance, eternity, etc.), if someone strives to explain such things by notions of this kind, which are only aids of the imagination, he will accomplish nothing more than if he takes pains to go mad with his imagination. (Ep. 12; G IV, 57)

In other words, should one confine oneself to sense experience alone, metaphysics – or, to put it more bluntly, *philosophy* – is simply impossible.

In the *Ethics*, Spinoza famously makes a three-tiered distinction in order to explicate the nature and position of the different kinds of cognition in his top-down approach. In this section, we focus on what Spinoza considers the lowest kind of knowledge, according to which we perceive things either (a) "from singular things which have been represented to us through the senses in a way that is mutilated, confused, and without order for the intellect (see p29c)" or (b) "from signs, e.g., from the fact that, having heard or read certain words, we recollect things, and form certain ideas of them, which are like them, and through which we imagine the things (p18s)" (2p40s2). Spinoza ends by declaring: "These two ways of regarding things I shall henceforth call knowledge of the first kind, opinion or imagination" (E2p40s2). *Imagination* is thus the term with which Spinoza refers to the most ordinary cases of sense perception (such as seeing a cat in front of oneself) – which, as noted, occupy the lowest tier in his epistemology.

We will soon return to the classificatory framework of the *Ethics*. For the present purposes, it should be noted that it does not come out of nowhere but strongly reflects the one presented in the early methodological work, the *Treatise on the Emendation of the Intellect*.[18] In it, Spinoza states that "all the modes of perceiving" (TIE, §18) can be reduced "to four main kinds." Here are the first two:

1 There is the perception we have from report or from some conventional sign.
2 There is the perception we have from random experience, that is, from experience that is not determined by the intellect. But it has this name only because it comes to us by chance, and we have no other experiment that opposes it. So it remains with us unshaken. (TIE, §19)

The first two kinds clearly match imagination, the lowest type of knowledge of the *Ethics*. In the TIE, Spinoza not only illustrates in a helpful manner this type of cognition; he also evaluates its significance in our lives:

> I know only from report my date of birth, and who my parents were, and similar things [...]. By random experience I know that I shall die, for I affirm this because I have seen others like me die [...]. Again, I also know by random experience that oil is capable of feeding fire, and that water is capable of putting it out. I know also that the dog is a barking animal, and man a rational one. And *in this way I know almost all the things that are useful in life.* (TIE, §20, emphasis added)

In other words, the low epistemic status does not mean that the information from reports or adventitious sense experience – however inadequate – would not be most useful for practical purposes, such as finding nourishment and shelter.

Now we have some idea about what Spinoza means by sense perception and its status in his system. But *why* is sense perception so "mutilated" and "confused" and hence inadequate? To answer this question, we must return to, and elaborate on, Spinoza's view of the mind–body union. Recall that the human mind has the body as its object and so perceives everything that happens in the body. *Sense perception is about our mind perceiving* – one could perhaps say *registering – the way in which an external body affects our body.* This process inevitably involves at least two entities, our body and the external body (or bodies), which has a major impact on the epistemic nature of sense perception. Here is how Spinoza describes the issue:

> The idea of any mode in which the human body is affected by external bodies must involve the nature of the human body and at the same time the nature of the external body (2p16).

> For all the modes in which a body is affected follow from the nature of the affected body, and at the same time from the nature of the affecting body (by a1"). So the idea of them (by 1a4) will necessarily involve the nature of each body. And so the idea of each mode in which the human body is affected by an external body involves the nature of the human body and of the external body. (2p16d)

This is perhaps an unnecessarily complicated way of expressing a simple point: since we form ideas of external objects as they affect our body, it is of course understandable that the idea of the resulting affection involves both our body and the external body (or bodies). This prompts Spinoza to state that "the ideas which we have of external bodies *indicate the condition of our own body more than the nature of external bodies*" (2p16c2, emphasis added). In other words, when Peter has a sense perception of, for instance, a horse, that perception is *more about Peter's body* than it is about the horse.[19] Given this, it should come as no surprise that sense perception *of the external object* is, for Spinoza, inadequate: "The idea of any affection of the human body does not involve adequate knowledge of an external body" (2p25). Consistently enough, the same holds for the ideas we have of our own body: "The human mind does not involve adequate knowledge of the parts composing the human body" (2p24). Again, Spinoza's official line of argument is decidedly God-driven. The following passage draws on the aforementioned propositions and offers perhaps the best summary of Spinoza's mindset:

> [T]he ideas of the affections of the human body involve the nature of external bodies as much as that of the human body (by p16), and must involve the nature not only of the human body [NS: as a whole], but also of its parts; for the affections are modes (by po3) with which the parts of the human body, and consequently the whole body, are affected. But (by p24 and p25) *adequate knowledge of external bodies and of the parts composing the human body is in God, not insofar as he is considered to be affected with the human mind, but insofar as he is considered to be affected with other ideas.* Therefore, these ideas of the affections, insofar as they are related only to the human mind, are like conclusions without premises, i.e. [...] they are confused ideas. (2p28d, emphasis added)

This connects to what we discussed earlier in the chapter: when for instance Mary perceives something, what from the Spinozistically adequate viewpoint happens is that God *qua* Mary perceives something. And the line between adequacy and inadequacy of ideas is drawn precisely at the latter, fundamental register: "[W]hen we say that God has this or that idea, not only insofar as he constitutes the nature of the human mind, but insofar as he also has the idea of another thing together with the human mind, then we say that the human mind perceives the thing only partially, *or* inadequately" (2p11c). The point is that God can only have adequate ideas,[20] and when God has an idea through our mind *alone, our* idea is adequate; but when God has an idea through several things, our mind being one of them, our idea is inadequate.[21] In itself, Spinoza's reasoning is relatively easy to grasp: cognition of any thing requires cognition of its cause(s) (1a4); now assuming that our mind cognizes only some, not all, of the causes of the effect which is an affection of our body and the concomitant idea in our mind, that idea cannot but be cognitively deficient.

Given that Spinoza's way of arguing might strike us as overly divinity-laden, we suggest that his point can be also be given the following, quite mundane, gloss. According to him, sense perceptions are just affections produced through interactions with external objects, the ideas of which reveal more of our body than the external bodies, resulting in fragmentary knowledge, which can only be inadequate. Moreover, the respective contribution of each element is difficult if not altogether impossible to distinguish phenomenologically. This is why the idea cannot but be a confused mix of at least two dissimilar but indistinguishable elements. All this explains why Spinoza states that "[f]alsity consists in the privation of knowledge which inadequate, *or* mutilated and confused, ideas involve" (2p35).

4.4 Adequate knowledge

According to Spinoza, there are two main kinds of adequate cognition. Spinoza labels the lower of these, i.e., the second kind of knowledge, *reason* (*ratio*). It arises "from the fact that we have common notions and adequate ideas of the properties of things (see p38c, p39, p39c, and p40)" (2p40s2). As the reference to the preceding propositions signals, here Spinoza invokes his doctrine of *common notions*. The argument ultimately relies on 2p38, which reads: "Those things which are common to all, and which are equally in the part and in the whole, can only be conceived adequately." Here is the demonstration:

> Let A be something which is common to all bodies, and which is equally in the part of each body and in the whole. I say that A can only be conceived adequately. For its idea (by p7c) will necessarily be adequate in God, both insofar as he has the idea of the human body and insofar as he has ideas of its affections, which (by p16, p25, and p27) involve in part both the nature of the human body and that of external bodies. That is (by p12 and p13), this idea will necessarily be adequate in God insofar as he constitutes the human mind, or insofar as he has ideas that are in the human mind. The mind therefore (by p11c) necessarily perceives A adequately, and does so both insofar as it perceives itself and insofar as it perceives its own or any external body. Nor can A be conceived in another way. (2p38d)

While it is clear that the argument states that the ideas we have in common with other minds are adequate because God can have adequate ideas *qua* our mind *alone*, it does little to elucidate the all-important connection between commonality and adequacy. The point that there are things "equally in the part of each body and in the whole" may be found helpful but hardly throws sufficient light on the matter. Spinoza's reasoning seems to turn on the idea that certain features common to all things are *uniform and not composed of parts* – this is why they can be called "common" to begin with – and so any idea of them is as accurate and correct as the next one. This is something Descartes very informatively explicates in the twelfth rule of his early *Rules for the Direction of the Mind*:

> [S]ince we are concerned here with things only in so far as they are perceived by the intellect, *we term "simple" only those things which we know so clearly and distinctly that they cannot be divided by the mind into others which are more distinctly known. Shape, extension and motion, etc. are of this sort; all the rest we conceive to be in a sense composed out of these.* (CSM I, 44, emphasis added)

> [T]hese simple natures are all self-evident and never contain any falsity. [...] For it can happen that we think we are ignorant of things we really know, as for example when we suspect that they contain something else which eludes us, something beyond what we intuit or reach in our thinking, even though we are mistaken in thinking this. For this reason, it is evident that we are mistaken if we ever judge that we lack complete knowledge of any one of these simple natures. *For if we have even the slightest grasp of it in our mind – which we surely must have, on the assumption that we are making a judgement about it – it must follow that we have complete knowledge of it. Otherwise it could not be said to be simple,* but a composite made up of that which we perceive in it and that of which we judge we are ignorant. (CSM I, 45, emphasis added)

Correspondingly, Spinoza's basic thesis concerning common properties is quite straightforward: there are properties common to all individuals – such as being extended or in motion – absolutely *uniform* so that *either one grasps them clearly and distinctly or not at all.*[22] For instance, if Peter perceives a cat and a tree in front of him, he cannot misperceive the cat's and the tree's extendedness (that is, having breadth, width, and height); extension is such a homogeneous thing that whenever it is perceived, it is necessarily perceived adequately – as a common notion.[23] Arguably, the first principles of the *Ethics* are in a similar fashion simple and self-evident but still so fecund that when conjoined they can give rise to more complex conclusions – ultimately to an entire philosophical system.

Finally, there is the third and highest kind of knowledge: *intuitive* knowledge. Spinoza defines it as follows: "[T]his kind of knowing proceeds from an adequate idea of the formal essence of certain attributes of God to the adequate knowledge of the [NS: formal] essence of things" (2p40s2). Ever since its introduction, this kind of knowledge has been found to be something of a mystery. Spinoza himself gives us the following illustration:

> Suppose there are three numbers, and the problem is to find a fourth which is to the third as the second is to the first. Merchants do not hesitate to multiply the second by the third, and divide the product by the first, because they have not yet forgotten what they heard from their teacher without any demonstration, or because they have often found this in the simplest numbers, or from the force of the Demonstration of p7 in Bk. VII of Euclid, viz. from the common property of proportionals. But in the simplest numbers none of this is necessary. Given the numbers 1, 2, and 3, no one fails to see that the fourth proportional number is 6 – and we see this much more clearly because we infer the fourth number from the ratio which, in one glance, we see the first number to have the second. (2p40s2)

While there is much that remains unclear about this example, one thing seems nevertheless beyond doubt: there is something markedly *direct* or *immediate* about the third kind of knowledge, whereby it is intuitive in a way that other forms of knowledge are not. Moreover, the highest kind of knowledge is strictly faithful to the top-down model: it begins with God's (essence-constituting) attributes and proceeds to the essences of (infinite and finite) things or modifications.

The precursor of intuitive knowledge is quite clearly the highest kind of knowledge presented in the TIE, namely "the perception we have when a thing is perceived through its essence alone, or through knowledge of its proximate cause" (TIE, §19). This kind of knowledge "comprehends the adequate essence of the thing and is without danger of error" (TIE, §29). Thus, even though the classification of the TIE differs, at least as far as the highest kinds of knowledge are concerned, from the one presented in the *Ethics*, we should note that even in the earlier work Spinoza emphasizes the role of essences in adequate knowledge formation. Clear and distinct ideas of things are thus first and foremost about their *essences*.

Grasping such knowledge intuitively definitely seems like a tall order. However, there are ways to spell out the core idea. Here is one way, drawing on what Spinoza writes in the TIE.

Recall that intuitive knowledge begins with an attribute of God. *Extension* is an attribute of God and, as we have noted, we can either know it adequately or not at all. So we have the adequate idea of extension, or of three-dimensional space, on which to base our further cognitive efforts.[24] So let us combine extension with another common property of which we can only have an adequate cognition and put a point (a simple thing if anything is) into recti-linear *motion*: we inevitably arrive at an idea of a line – perhaps the most basic of all *shapes*, which, according to Descartes on whom Spinoza is drawing on these matters, count among simple things. Next let us keep one end of the line fixed while we move the other[25]; the result is, as we immediately and intuitively understand, a circle. Finally, if we rotate the circle around its diameter, we have arrived, beginning from the attribute of extension and by combining such common things as motion and shapes, quite intuitively at what forms the very essence of a sphere.[26]

Indeed, Spinoza's theory of truth concerning complex ideas focuses first and foremost on the way in which the essences of their objects are constituted, as opposed to how we happen to encounter things. Here is an example of this line of thought: "[I]f some architect conceives a building in an orderly fashion, then although such a building never existed, and even never will exist, still the thought of it is true, and the thought is the same, whether the building exists or not" (TIE, §69). Of course, in the ontology of the *Ethics*, there are, as we have seen, no genuine unrealized possibil-ities, for God or Nature produces everything it understands[27]; hence we can be sure that any genuinely possible existent is real. All this well displays Spinoza's extreme epistemic optimism: he appears to be confident that there is no reason to think that gaining intuitive knowledge of even very complex things (such as the human body) would *in principle* be out of our reach, as our knowledge of nature progresses. Moreover, as we will later see,[28] the doctrine of intuitive knowledge not only connects to but is the very basis of the capstone of Spinoza's ethical thought, according to which we view the universe from a timeless perspective.

4.5 Belief formation

From 2p45 to 2p47, Spinoza argues that because each idea of body involves an idea of an eternal and infinite essence of God, namely, extension, the mind has "an adequate knowledge of God's eternal and infinite essence" (2p47). Since he also claims that "[one] who has an adequate idea [...] must at the same time have an adequate idea, *or* true knowledge, of his own knowledge" (2p43), Spinoza is left to answer why people appear not to be aware of this adequate knowledge of God's eternal extended essence. Spinoza's response is to maintain that while people do have adequate knowledge of God's essence, they "do not rightly explain their own mind," attaching the name "God" to images derived from things that they have experienced. His point here seems to be that our adequate understanding of God is obscured by the anthropomorphic images that we have associated with the idea. This reveals something important about Spinoza's conception of mind: one can *have* an idea without being able to grasp it very consciously or report it very accurately. This is not because there are ideas that are dormant or inert since, for Spinoza, to exist is to exert some power (1p36). Rather, ideas may be overshadowed by other ideas, as when the confused ideas that we have attached to the name "God" prevent us from fully accessing our true idea of God. The *power* of an idea determines what we think about most and how we think about it. And, indeed, the power of an idea determines the grade of belief or level of epistemic commitment.

To appreciate what is distinctive about Spinoza's account of epistemic commitment and belief formation, we should first consider how his view differs from the Cartesian alternative. In the Fourth Meditation, Descartes seeks to make sense of why he is prone to form mistaken judgments despite the fact that every-thing in him comes from a non-deceiving God. He maintains that judgment arises through the concurrence of two faculties: the intellect, or the "faculty of understanding," and the will. The faculty of the understanding supplies the content for judgment, while the will takes a stance in relation to that content – affirming it, denying it, or suspending judgment. It is as if the understanding is a clerk that supplies a report to the executive (i.e., the will), who can accept it, reject it, or withhold judgment until further information comes to light. Error arises because there is a mismatch of scope between the two faculties: while the human understanding is neces-sarily "extremely slight and very limited," the will is "formally and precisely" as unlimited as God's (CSM II, 40, translation modified) – it can affirm, deny, or suspend judgment in relation to *any* content, no matter how poorly understood it is. So, for Descartes, we humans make mistaken judgments only when we misuse our will, affirming or denying things that we do not fully grasp. And we cannot blame

God for endowing us with faculties with mismatched scope, for while a finite, human understanding is necessarily limited, the very concept of a will is something that is unbounded – one cannot have half a will, as it were.

Spinoza rejects nearly this entire picture. In keeping with his necessitarianism, he denies that we have a free will (2p48), claiming further that "the understanding" and "the will" are "either complete fictions or nothing but metaphysical beings, or universals" (2p48s), which he previously claimed to be confused representations of a collection of particulars (2p40s1). Strictly speaking, there are no general faculties of mind, only particular ideas. This fits with his critique of traditional philosophical theology,[29] specifically his claim that theological problems arise because people take the will and intellect to be a part of God's essence. Spinoza rejects this view, claiming instead that "[t]he will, like the intellect, is only a certain mode of thinking" (1p32d) and, as modes of thought, must be determined to exist and act.

In the concluding propositions of the second part of the *Ethics*, Spinoza examines more directly the relations between ideas and volitions as particular modes of thinking, concluding that "singular volitions and ideas are one and the same" (2p49cd). The reasoning in support of the view that ideas and volitions are "one and the same" thing is far from clear. Spinoza argues first that volitions – understood here as this or that affirmation (or negation) – can neither be nor be conceived without the idea. In short, there must be some *idea* that is being affirmed or denied. However, he then proceeds to make the rather more contestable claim that ideas themselves can neither be nor be conceived without an affirmation or negation. Ideas possess an intrinsic volitional power – they are intrinsically belief-like, as it were. As opposed to the Cartesian picture of belief, exemplified through the model of the clerk and executive above, on the Spinozist view there is no report-gathering faculty (e.g., understanding) and no executive faculty (e.g., faculty of will) that signs off on the report; ideas arise with stamps of approval (or disapproval) already inscribed, as it were. Taking this point together with the claim that volitions always presuppose some idea, Spinoza concludes that where there is a volition, there is an idea, and where there is an idea, there is a volition. Volitions pertain to the very essence of idea (2p49d, 2p49s; G II, 134). On the basis of the tight connection between essences and things, Spinoza infers directly that volitions are "one and the same thing" as ideas.

The crucial claim point here is that ideas are intrinsically dynamic.[30] According to Spinoza, just as bodies are not inert, but have an intrinsic force,[31] ideas are not like "mute pictures on a panel" (2p49s), but have their own form of activity. Affirmation and negation are to ideas what motion and rest are to bodies: pervasive properties that explain why the things that they characterize do what they do. By defining ideas as concepts rather than perceptions (2def3), Spinoza stresses the active, volitional aspect of modes of thinking.[32] Affirmation in particular has a kind of pride of place: to have an idea is to affirm something. All ideas are belief-like; they posit their object and hold onto it until disposed otherwise: "If the human body is affected with a mode that involves the nature of an external body, the human mind will regard the same external body as actually existing, or as present to it, *until the body is affected by an affect that excludes the existence or presence of that body*" (2p17, emphasis added).

But if all ideas are belief-like, how does one come to doubt or disbelieve something? Spinoza answers this question in his response to the Cartesian objection that belief *must* involve the faculty of will since one can "feign" a winged horse without believing that it exists (2p49s; G II, 132–3). He claims that if a child had the idea of a winged horse without any other idea, he *would* believe a winged horse exists (2p49s; G II, 134). Doubt and disbelief arise only because we form further ideas whose content offsets the idea of the winged horse:

> [I]f the mind perceived nothing else except the winged horse, it would regard it as present to itself, and would not have any cause of doubting its existence [...] unless either the imagination of the winged horse were joined to an idea which excluded the existence of the same horse, or the mind perceived that its idea of a winged horse was inadequate. And then either it will necessarily deny the horse's existence, or it will necessarily doubt it. (2p49s; G II, 134)

The claim that denial occurs only when the initial idea is joined with a further idea that excludes it raises the question of what exactly *exclusion* consists in. As Diane Steinberg has pointed out, it cannot merely be a logical notion since two ideas with incompatible content (p and ~p) equally exclude one another logically,[33] while the form of exclusion that Spinoza describes above is asymmetrical: the idea that excludes the idea of the winged horse – e.g., the testimony of a parent that winged horses do not exist – is not itself excluded.

Rather, it must be that one idea excludes another only when these ideas have incompatible content *and* the former has more causal power than another. This fits with claims that Spinoza makes later in the *Ethics*, where he explains exclusion in terms of the power of ideas, as when he writes: "[I]maginations do not disappear through the presence of the true insofar as it is true, but because there occur others, *stronger than them*, which exclude the present existence of the things we imagine" (4p1s, emphasis added).

So, all ideas are belief-like, but only those ideas that are not offset, or excluded, by other, more powerful, ideas direct our minds. This account can be illustrated through Spinoza's example of the two ideas of the sun.[34] Spinoza claims that anyone who perceives the sun represents it as near, insofar as one's body is affected in a certain way. However, while one cannot but perceive or imagine the sun as nearby, one can simultaneously have an idea of the sun's true distance that is strong enough to overpower the imagination's representation. Because of this, even though one's perception of the sun involves affirming it as close, this non-veridical idea does not lead to false belief, provided that one also possesses a stronger excluding idea of the true distance (2p35s, 4p1s). As he puts it, "the mind does not err from the fact that it imagines, but only insofar as it is considered to lack an idea which excludes the existence of those things which it imagines to be present to it" (2p17s).[35] This supports the more general thesis that when one has conflicting ideas, it is the more powerful idea that expresses one's belief.[36]

This view of ideas vying for dominance over the mind captures the spirit of the *Ethics* as a whole, which is concerned with emending our minds and gaining control over our wayward ideas and passions, not through the exercise of a radically free will but by ramping up the power of our knowledge and diminishing the power of the confused representations of the imagination.[37] Returning to the idea of God that Spinoza thinks that we all necessarily have, we need to find ways to minimize the power of confused images that prevents the true idea from shining through.

To conclude, it is worth noting that Spinoza's view of belief formation has gained recent adherents in psychology and philosophy of cognition. Psychologist Daniel Gilbert was among the first to defend the so-called "Spinozan" view of belief formation, taking the view to be comprised of two doctrines: the Unity Hypothesis, according to which to understand an idea is to accept it in the first instance, and the Asymmetry Hypothesis, according to which "the rejection of an idea occurs subsequent to, and more effortfully than, its acceptance."[38] Gilbert shows how a range of research from social, cognitive, and developmental psychology – including studies that he designed specifically to test these hypotheses – supports the view that the default cognitive stance is that of acceptance and that doubt and disbelief are secondary stances that require greater cognitive effort. If this view is right, humans are credulous by nature, prone to immediately accepting what we read and hear and to retain traces of past beliefs even after they have been debunked. The social and political implications of this account are significant and potentially disturbing: we are highly susceptible to propaganda and to fabricated (or fake) news, especially when we are cognitively depleted.[39] Spinoza himself seems to have been aware of these troubling implications, leading him to write political works that are attentive to the ways that social conditions affect the spread of misinformation and that seek to build in protections against these threats.[40]

Further reading

Della Rocca, Michael. 1996. *Representation and the Mind–Body Problem in Spinoza*. New York: Oxford University Press.

Garrett, Don. 2018. *Nature and Necessity in Spinoza's Philosophy*. Oxford: Oxford University Press, chs 5–7, 14–15.

Marshall, Eugene. 2013. *The Spiritual Automaton: Spinoza's Science of the Mind*. Oxford: Oxford University Press.

Renz, Ursula. 2018. *The Explainability of Experience: Realism and Subjectivity in Spinoza's Theory of the Human Mind*. Oxford: Oxford University Press.

Steinberg, Diane. 2009. "Knowledge in Spinoza's *Ethics*," in Olli Koistinen (ed.), *The Cambridge Companion to Spinoza's* Ethics, pp. 140–66. Cambridge: Cambridge University Press.

Wilson, Margaret D. 1996. "Spinoza's Theory of Knowledge," in Don Garrett (ed.), *The Cambridge Companion to Spinoza*, pp. 89–141. Cambridge: Cambridge University Press.

5

Action and Emotion

At the dawn of the seventeenth century, the dominant Aristotelian theory of action was decidedly teleological. According to this line of thought, human beings act for the sake of certain ends. And indeed, to this very day it is difficult to avoid the idea that we are purposive agents and as such in some basic sense end-directed – even though few conceive of that directedness in classically teleological terms. Thus it is understandable that although teleological explanations of natural phenomena began to diminish even before the birth of the new science, the role of "ends" in explaining the behavior of cognitive entities remained largely unchallenged. As we have seen,[1] for the scholastics, God is a purposive cognitive agent *par excellence*, an agent with the power to execute what he freely wills, who brings into existence a world of natural agents with ends. In this framework, a *full* explanation of the universe thus must appeal to the *ends* or *purposes* of a human-like creator. But as is now clear, Spinoza is decidedly against this view and spills much ink to combat it. It is thus no surprise that there is a strong consensus among the scholars that Spinoza discards what may be called *divine teleology*. However, as far as human behavior is concerned, at least certain kinds of teleological explanations seem inescapable: what could be more obvious than the fact that we do things *in order to* bring about things we want or desire? Still, if one takes teleological explanations to be distinct from mechanistic explanations, or final causes to be distinct from efficient causes, it seems that Spinoza rejects teleological explanations more generally.[2] The unquestionable basis of Spinoza's (arguably novel) theory of motivation and emotion is the so-called conatus principle: "Each thing, insofar as it is in itself, strives to persevere in its being" (3p6, translation modified). We will begin this chapter with a thorough analysis of that principle and its most immediate consequences. In the ensuing sections, we show how it not only overturns what were the prevailing ways of understanding human behavior but we also outline and discuss the bold theory of emotions Spinoza builds on it.[3]

5.1 The conatus principle and its context

When Spinoza arrives on the scene, the view that animate things naturally strive to preserve themselves had for centuries been part and parcel of western philosophy, most importantly through the teachings of Stoics, for whom the impulse (*hormê*) to self-preservation forms the basis of a naturalistic ethics. What is more, Spinoza begins his ethical theorizing by telling us how our basic striving is manifested as desire and will (3p9s) *before* discussing such notions as virtue and the good (4def1 and def8) – thereby proceeding precisely in the order customary in ancient moral philosophy, naturalistic in its basic orientation, where ethical theorizing was to begin with psychology and not with ethical ideals.

These affinities with ancient theories notwithstanding, the breakthrough of the new mechanical sciences radically altered the intellectual landscape by Spinoza's time: most importantly, the teleological view of the way in which the world and things in it were ordered was under strong pressures, to which Spinoza was clearly quite sensitive. In brief, naturalistic ethics had to be rethought given the dubiousness of final ends. The way in which Spinoza's conatus principle, cited above, is formulated betrays its debt to the Cartesian first law of nature, which reads: "[E]ach thing, insofar as it is in itself, always continues in the same state" (*Principles* II.37; CSM I, 240, translation modified). It also seems to echo Hobbes's metaphysics, according to which everything is ultimately explicable in terms of motion, the small beginnings of which is conatus (EW I.6). Neither of these doctrines contains anything teleological in their basic elements. Together with Spinoza's ardent denial of divine teleology (1app), this gives one reason to think that Spinoza believed the conatus theory to be, in its essentials, unencumbered by teleological metaphysics. That he might well be right about this does not mean that the issue of teleology would thereby be over and done with, as we will see in what follows. At any rate, the proper context of the conatus theory is not hard to discern; it stems from a long and venerable tradition concerning the natural operations of things. This should not be taken to mean that Spinoza would here be somehow unoriginal. Already from the outset, it is clear that his approach is radical in the way it takes elements from doctrines pertaining to the material world and animate entities and applies them to *everything* in Nature: the conatus principle is a completely general metaphysical principle, applying to all finite things of all attributes.

The crucial twin propositions – 3p6 and 3p7 – are written in Spinoza's trademark condensed style, which increases the interpretative challenge. Here we should pay attention not only to their argumentative ancestry, referred to in their demonstrations, but also to their progeny, especially to what Spinoza takes himself to be entitled to derive directly from them. To a significant degree, 3p6 is the nexus through which certain key tenets of the opening part of the *Ethics* find their way to the latter part of the work. Its demonstration reads:

> For singular things are modes by which God's attributes are expressed in a certain and determinate way (by 1p25c), i.e. (by 1p34), things that express, in a certain and determinate way, God's power, by which God is and acts. And no thing has anything in itself by which it can be destroyed, or which takes its existence away (by p4). On the contrary, it is opposed to everything which can take its existence away (by p5). Therefore, as far as it can, and it is in itself [*quantum potest, et in se est*], it strives to persevere in its being. (3p6, translation modified)

The demonstration, which consists of four elements, has been the topic of a lively discussion. Jonathan Bennett (1984: ch. 10) famously accused Spinoza of committing a number of fallacies in deriving this doctrine. This marked the starting point of the discussion[4]; but it should be noted that Bennett also set its orientation in the sense that, in the discussion that ensued, Spinoza was widely seen to derive 3p6 from the immediately preceding conceptual considerations (i.e., 3p4 and 3p5) *alone*. Perhaps because the notion of power – long in disrepute – has recently been rehabilitated in analytic metaphysics, the beginning of the demonstration invoking God's power does not feel as problematic, or otiose, as it once did.[5] At any rate, that the demonstration builds on Spinoza's dynamistic tendencies seems nowadays to be widely, and sympathetically, acknowledged. Obviously, we are dealing with *a power that strives against opposition,* and that power certainly must, in Spinoza's framework, have God as its source. It seems obvious that Spinoza combines 1p25c with 1p34 to claim that finite *expressions* of an essentially powerful or causally efficacious God are endowed with conatus. He seems to think that the very notion of expression brings with it the idea that expressions (here: finite things) retain the basic character of what they express (here: God). Thus, given that God is essentially powerful, expressions must be so too – simply to qualify as genuine expressions.

If one does not find this convincing enough, it should be noted that 3p4 and 3p5 reflect two much earlier basic propositions, namely 1p11 and 1p16. Just as in 1p11d2, Spinoza argues that God's nonexistence would imply the absurdity that its "nature would involve contradiction," he proves 3p4 by claiming that "the definition of any thing affirms, and does not deny, the thing's essence, *or* it posits the thing's essence, and does not take it away" (3p4d). In other words, whether we are dealing with God or finite things, the essence of a thing cannot destroy the thing. If it could, that would mean that we were not dealing with a genuine essence and definition at all. 3p5, in turn, can be perceived as echoing 1p16, as it says that entities (or properties) of a contrary nature cannot be in the same subject (or thing); it thus invokes the very same thing–property structure as 1p16 does, only this time in terms general enough to apply to finite things as well. Read from this angle, 3p4 and 3p5 thus latch onto the very same essence–property ontology that underpins the claim that God is essentially powerful and which we have seen Spinoza endorse.[6] So it is no wonder that Spinoza thinks that finite things are powerful just in the same basic sense that God is.

Even if the argument for the conatus principle were not as airtight as some would like, the preceding shows that, within his framework, Spinoza has solid grounds to think that he has given his readers enough reasons to endorse the principle. The next point he wants to drive home is that it is no garden-variety feature of things: "The striving by which each thing strives to persevere in its being is nothing but the actual essence of the thing" (3p7). In other words, things are *strivers by their very essence or nature*. For Spinoza's intended audience, the appearance of the notion of essence is hardly a surprise: after all, the previous proposition states that any thing strives to persevere in its being *insofar as it is in itself* (*quantum in se est*), and this phrase was in Spinoza's time used to refer to what things do "according to their nature."[7] Moreover, keeping in mind that the concept of essence figures in the immediate ancestry of the conatus principle (3p4d), the ground is already prepared for introducing the notion of essence. In 3p7d, the passage in which Spinoza does that, he first reminds us that things are causally efficacious, or powerful, by their essences alone (by 1p29 and 1p36); thus, as power, striving is equated with the essence of things. The essence in question is precisely the *actual* essence (*essentia actualis*) presumably because conatus is the power at play in constantly varying circumstances of *temporal* existence – the contrast being with the unchanging and eternal formal essence (*essentia formalis*) of things.[8] In other words, if little of what Spinoza says in the opening part of the *Ethics* involves anything temporal, the conatus principle specifies the way in which intrinsically powerful finite things act under the constant influence of other finite things or, to put it in Spinoza's idiom, "external causes."

5.2 Main features of finite things as strivers

With regard to the progeny of the conatus propositions, we would now like to highlight three elemental points that make their presence felt through the rest of the *Ethics*, the significance and ramifications of which we will explore in greater detail in the ensuing sections.

First, examining the grounds for the claim that our mind strives both insofar as it has inadequate and adequate ideas (3p9) leads us to the notion of *desire*, which, is a – or perhaps even *the* – key element in Spinoza's theory of action. Spinoza defends this proposition by pointing out that "[t]he essence of the mind is constituted by adequate and inadequate ideas" (3p9d). The idea here is that under the influence of external causes, our actual essence is continually *constituted* anew, which, given that our essence is striving, results in corresponding changes in our causal efficacy. This topic has received much too little attention in the literature, but we think that it would be hard to overstate its importance.[9] The very first definition of affects explains that "by the word *desire* I understand any of a man's strivings, impulses, appetites, and volitions, which vary as the man's constitution varies, and which are not infrequently so opposed to one another that the man is pulled in different directions and knows not where to turn" (defaff1). Clearly, Spinoza is sensitive to the fact that our existence is often a troubled affair, and the doctrine of striving as desire forms an important part of his view of the dynamics of actual existence.

Desire, one of the three basic human emotions,[10] is the striving "related to the mind and body together" of which we are conscious

(3p9s). And *the actual constitution of the essence* determines our desire: "[D]esire is the very essence, *or* nature, of each [man] insofar as it conceived to be determined, by whatever constitution he has, to do something" (3p56d). All this seems to take place with the same necessity we find in geometry; much of what Spinoza writes later in the third part of the *Ethics* about our actions and emotions has as its paradigm the way in which a certain property (e.g., fulfilling the Pythagorean theorem) follows from the essence of a figure constituted in a certain way (e.g., a triangle that is right-angled). In any case, the notion of constitution of essences is obviously designed to explain how a thing can remain numerically the same (the essence remains unaltered) while undergoing numerous changes (the constitutions vary). But perhaps even a more significant consequence of all this is that particular desires are determined by different constitutions of a thing's essence. We will later explicate the precise way in which essences are constituted.[11]

Second, striving is intimately linked to what is *good* for us: "From all this, then, it is clear that we neither strive for, nor will, neither want, nor desire anything because we judge it to be good; on the contrary, we judge something to be good because we strive for it, will it, want it, and desire it (3p9s)."[12] It is not altogether clear what the "all this" is from which this should be clear; presumably, that willing, desiring, and so on are all forms of conatus introduced a few propositions earlier, but there is no shortage of interpretative leeway. However, it would be, we think, very difficult to deny that here Spinoza goes decidedly against one central feature of traditional teleological models, namely against what may be called the thesis of *intrinsic normativity*. According to Spinoza, people mistakenly believe in final causes as independent goods because they maintain "that the gods direct all things for the use of men" (1app). In other words, Spinoza sees such final causes as part and parcel of a misguided providential worldview in which God has a grand plan,[13] very much centered on the welfare of human beings, which dictates that there are intrinsically good things "for the sake of which he [God] willed to prepare the means" (1app). In this framework, given the ends chosen by God, things with natures suitable to produce those ends must be created. In this brand of essentialism, *final causes as intrinsic goods* are *ontologically prior* to essences, for they determine the kind of essences there must be. But Spinoza's essentialism is of a decidedly different type: God's production of finite things as modifications involves no choice or planning, and the essence of those modifications, in turn, is the striving that manifests itself as desires and appetites, depending on the way in which a particular striving essence is constituted. Once the constitution is in place, the desire necessarily results and its object is judged good. Thus, "[w]hat is called a final cause is nothing but a human appetite insofar as it is considered as a principle, *or* primary cause, of some thing" (4pref); *our striving determines what is judged to be good* in the first place.[14]

Third, Spinoza signals that the conatus principle amounts to what may be called *power enhancement*. This is expressed in 3p12 and 3p13, which are not only notable in themselves but also the veritable testing stone for any interpretation of the conatus doctrine. They read as follows:

> The mind as far as it can, strives to imagine those things that increase or aid the body's power of acting. (3p12)

> When the mind imagines those things that diminish or restrain the body's power of acting, it strives, as far as it can, to recollect things which exclude their existence. (3p13)

What does he have in mind here? Let us take a look at the argument for the latter proposition:

> So long as the mind imagines anything of this kind, the power both of mind and of body is diminished or restrained (as we have demonstrated in p12); nevertheless, the mind will continue to imagine this thing until it imagines something else that excludes the thing's present existence (by 2p17), that is (as we have just shown), the power both of mind and of body is diminished or restrained until the mind imagines something else that excludes the existence of this thing; so the mind (by p9), as far as it can, will strive to imagine or recollect that other thing. (3p13d)

The demonstration begins by reminding us that the power of mind and body go hand in hand. The middle part of the demonstration states that when the mind thinks about something that decreases its power, it cannot but continue thinking about it unless there is something else that takes it away. As the reference to 2p17 indicates, this claim is based on the mechanist strain in Spinoza's psychology. The final part of the demonstration is the most interesting one: based on 3p9, which in turn is based on the conatus principle, the mind will strive to imagine that which opposes the thing which we think decreases our power. The claim is thus that our mind does not rest content continuing with the power-decreasing thought but strives to get rid of it. It is thus understandable that 3p12 and 3p13 are commonly read as saying that we strive to increase our power; however, it is worth stressing that the principle itself is reminiscent of the Cartesian law of motion that is about continuing in the prevailing motion, whatever it may be.

That conatus amounts to, in many if not most circumstances, striving for power-enhancement is confirmed by a much later definition central for Spinoza's whole ethical enterprise and with a direct reference to the conatus propositions: "By virtue and power I understand the same thing, that is (by 3p7), virtue, insofar as it is related to man, is the very essence, or nature, of man, insofar as he has the power of bringing about certain things, which can be understood through the laws of his nature alone" (4def8).

But things, or effects, "which can be understood through the laws" of a human being's nature *alone* are *actions*: "[W]e act when something happens, in us or outside us, of which we are the adequate cause, that is (by def1), when something in us or outside us *follows from our nature, which can be clearly and distinctly understood through it alone*" (3def2, emphasis added). The only conclusion to draw is that our striving is not merely about persevering in the prevailing state but about asserting our nature and what follows from it as much as possible. In fact, were this not true, it would be difficult to see on what Spinoza's ethical project, heavily stressing activity as it does, is based.[15]

5.3 Action and teleology

On the basis of the general conatus principle, Spinoza sets out to overturn familiar views of human action. As we have seen, much in the conatus doctrine revolves around natures or essences. We have also seen that the idea behind the claim that striving is our actual essence is that essences are causally efficacious, and the very same idea underpins the notions of desire and virtue. To put things in the least controversial terms, things as strivers constantly produce effects – that is, they constantly act in the non-technical sense of the term – and to the extent that those effects follow from their own nature alone, they are active, whereas when strivers produce effects in conjunction with other causes they are (at least somewhat) passive. Our analysis shows that Spinoza's theory of action contains two striking, and much more controversial, tenets.

First, everything we strive to do stems from the way in which our essence is constituted; a certain desire always corresponds to a certain constitution. The exact nature of our behavior – be that active or passive – depends on the prevailing constitution of our essence, which results in a specific desire that produces its effect if unhindered.

Second, finite things – human and nonhuman alike – strive to do more than just prolong their psychophysical existence; they *strive to be active*, that is, to produce effects that can be conceived through their own essence alone. They do this simply because from any given essence, considered in itself, certain effects follow or "flow" as properties. The model of causality that Spinoza has in mind here is the one provided by geometrical objects, from whose essence properties were seen to necessarily follow.[16] Sometimes Spinoza refers to this, quite appropriately given the philosophical tradition, as *emanation*.[17] Moreover, he clearly sees this as cohering with the essence–property ontology depicted above.

Indeed, the view that activity consists fundamentally in bringing about effects that follow from an essence allows Spinoza to account for human activity while rejecting the notion that we are pulled, as it were, by the intrinsic goodness of things. Of course, Spinoza admits that things can be called "good" – but this judgment of goodness depends on our striving, rather than the other way around (3p9s). But even if our essential striving determines what is good in the first place, one might well ask whether or not this kind of striving to realize one's own nature is teleological. It is *not* teleological in the traditional "full-blown" sense that ends would be involved in *structuring or determining our essences* (as they were in the Peripatetic framework where all things had their place in the grand providential plan); what we call ends are things that simply flow from our essences, those essences in turn being what they are because they follow from God's nature.

However, less robust senses of Spinozistic teleology have been presented and defended. If teleology is, for instance, understood *not* as a doctrine concerning the very *makeup of things* but merely as *a form of explanation* which "purports to explain an event, process, or state of affairs in terms of a likely or possible consequence of that event, process, or state of affairs,"[18] it would be difficult – and probably unnecessary – to deny that the conatus doctrine allows teleological explanations.[19] Most famously, "[w]e strive to further the occurrence of whatever we imagine will lead to joy, and to avert or destroy what we imagine is contrary to it, *or* will lead to sadness"

(3p28) seems rather straightforwardly to license explaining at least some of our strivings in terms of their consequences. What is distinctive about Spinoza's account, though, is that he is able to reconcile this minimal sense of teleology as *acting for the sake of something* with the essence–property model of causality by reducing final causes to appetites, or manifestations of one's striving. Thus, while there is still a lively scholarly debate concerning whether or not Spinoza endorses teleology, and if he does in what sense,[20] there can be no doubt that he at the very least profoundly problematizes the familiar teleological picture of human action.

5.4 Architecture of emotions

We noted above that desire is determined by the constitution of one's essence. But what exactly is a constitution of one's essence, and how does it determine desire? In the end of *Ethics* part 3, Spinoza claims that any affection is a constitution of our essence (defaff1; G II, 190). But he has in mind a particular subset of affections, namely, what he calls the *affects* (3def3), or emotions, by which he means "affections of the body by which the body's power of acting is increased or diminished, aided or restrained, and at the same time, the ideas of these affections" (3def3).[21] Returning once again to 3p56d, we see that joy and sadness determine desire:

> [D]esire is the very essence, *or* nature, of each [man] insofar as it is conceived to be determined, by whatever constitution he has, to do something (see p9s). Therefore, as each [man] is affected by external causes with this or that species of joy, sadness, love, hate, and so on, that is, as his nature is constituted in one way or the other, so his desires vary.[22]

To better understand what affects are and how emotions like joy and sadness relate to desire, it will be instructive to compare Spinoza's account to Descartes's.

Descartes's treatise on affects, *The Passions of the Soul*, was prompted by Princess Elisabeth's persistent inquiries into the mind–body relationship,[23] including her request that Descartes define the passions adequately.[24] Descartes complies, defining passions of the soul as perceptions that we relate to our soul rather than to external objects or our body (*Passions* I.23–5; CSM I, 336–8). To understand this distinction, imagine the following scenario. You enter a friend's home for dinner after a day of working outdoors in the winter. You see a fire in the living room and you smell appetizing food in the oven. These are perceptions of external objects. You feel the warmth of the fire on your body and a pang of hunger in your stomach. These are perceptions of your body. But this is not all that you perceive. You also perceive affection and gratitude for your friend. These are your passions.

But while, according to Descartes, passions refer to the soul, they are still in some respect related to the body and – at least typically – to external objects. They are connected to the body in the sense that they are "caused, maintained and strengthened by some movement of the [animal] spirits" (*Passions* I.27; CSM I, 339), the spirits being part of what we would nowadays call the nervous system. So, while the passions are mental states, they are produced and sustained by bodily activity, reflecting Descartes's commitment to body–mind causal interaction. Moreover, while they are *of* the soul, the passions are generally directed at some other object. To use contemporary language, passions are *intentional*: they are about something or someone. One feels love *for* one's friends, pity *for* an injured animal, anxiety *about* a test, and contempt *for* a bigot.

According to Descartes, passions also in some sense represent the value of their object (*Passions* II.42; CSM I, 349), and they do so in an exaggerated and unreliable way.[25] We must thus be vigilant not to have these representations "mislead the soul" (*Passions* III.211; CSM I, 403). In some passages at least, Descartes, like the Stoics before him,[26] suggests that passions represent value in virtue of being the effect of an evaluative judgment: "When we think of something as good with regard to us, i.e., as beneficial to us, this makes us have love for it; and when we think of it as evil or harmful, this arouses hatred in us [...][.] This same consideration of good and evil is the origin of all the other passions" (*Passions* II.56–7; CSM I, 350). Putting these components together, we may say that, for Descartes, passions are physically caused states of the soul that function as unreliable indicators of value and, at least sometimes, result from antecedent judgments of good and evil.[27] He maintains that there are six primitive or principal passions from which all the others arise: wonder, love, hatred, desire, joy, and sadness.

With the Cartesian picture in place, we can now better appreciate Spinoza's alternative. Spinoza sometimes treats affects as physical *and* mental, as when he defines them as "affections of the body [...] and at the same time, the ideas of these affections" (3def3). But he focuses on the mental aspect in *Ethics* part 3. Insofar as they are mental states, affects are doubly representational. In the first instance, they represent a change in the body. As he puts it, an affect is an "idea, by which the mind affirms of its body, or of some part of it, a greater or lesser force of existing than before" (gendefaff; G II, 203). As we have seen, "a mode of extension and the idea of that mode are one and the same thing, but expressed in two ways" (2p7s), and whatever happens in the body will be perceived by the mind (2p12–p13). Affects are thus how the mind represents changes in the body's power or acting or perfection. When the body becomes more powerful, we experience this as joy (*laetitia*), a positively valenced emotion (3p11s, defaff2); when the body diminishes in power, we experience this as sadness (*tristitia*), a negatively valenced emotion (3p11s, defaff3).

From this we see that Spinoza's account of affects reflects his understanding of the mind–body relationship, and its attendant critique of Cartesian dualism. Rather than claiming, as Descartes does, that affects are modes of thought that are caused by motions in the body – an account that Spinoza decries as "more occult than any occult quality" (5pref) – Spinoza thinks that, *qua* modes of thought, affects are, like all ideas, representations of the object of the mind, the body. As representations, they are conceptually distinct from bodily states; nevertheless, bodily changes and the mental representations of the changes are expressions of one and the same reality conceived in two different ways.

In addition to representing changes in one's body's power of acting, affects also represent some other object; in this way they are, just like Descartes's passions, intentional. As Spinoza puts it in 2a3, "[t]here are no modes of thinking, such as love, desire, or whatever is designated by the word affects of the mind, unless there is in the same individual the idea of the thing loved, desired, and the like." Typically, the object towards which an affect is directed is the thing that we imagine to have affected us or to have caused the change in our body's power of acting.

Like perceptual representation, then, affective representation is at once about one's own body and about the affecting thing. And affects acquire their character both from the nature of one's own body (3p57) and from the nature of the affecting bodies that we represent as the object of our emotion (3p56). As representations, affects have, in contemporary parlance, a mind-to-world direction of fit – that is, they seek to capture the world as it is. They can thus be assessed as apt, reasonable, misdirected, false, and so forth.

While Spinoza agrees with Descartes that affects are very often confused and unreliable, he advances a very different account of the relationship between affects and evaluative judgments. While Descartes thinks that one loves something because she judges it to be good and hates something because she judges it to be bad, Spinoza plainly rejects the explanatory priority of judgment. Instead – on our reading – he thinks that evaluative judgments are constituted by, and explained through, affects, claiming that the representation or cognition of good and evil is "nothing but an affect of joy or sadness, insofar as we are conscious of it" (4p8). While this is somewhat controversial as an interpretation, we think that the specific feature that constitutes the *evaluative* part of an affect is just its valence: whether it is positive or negative. To represent something as good is just to represent it lovingly or desirously; to represent something as evil is just to represent it hatefully or aversively. This helps to make sense of the provocative claim of 3p9s that "we neither strive for, nor will, neither want, nor desire anything because we judge it to be good; on the contrary, we judge something to be good because we strive for it, will it, want it, and desire it." Descartes and the Stoics are mistaken in supposing that there is an independent conception of what it means to represent value, which is distinct from – and explanatorily prior to – the affect. Spinoza's alternative is to think that affects themselves constitute evaluative judgments.[28]

In terms of the primary passions, Spinoza cuts Descartes's list in half, leaving only desire, joy, and sadness (see 3p11s).[29] His reason for dropping love and hatred seems to be that he regards these as derivative, as species of joy and sadness respectively.[30] His treatment of wonder is rather more complicated and more interesting. He agrees with Descartes that wonder fixes attention: "Wonder is an imagination of a thing in which the mind remains fixed because this singular imagination has no connection with the others" (defaff4).[31] But since, on this account, wonder on its own is just a mode of imagination, without any intrinsic valence, it is not, strictly speaking, an affect at all (defaff4exp). It can be joined with love or hatred, giving rise to the affects of veneration or disdain (3p52s, defaff4exp), but since neither love or hate are primary affects, neither are veneration or disdain. And whereas Descartes places wonder first among the passions (*Passions* II.53; CSM I, 350), as this passion calls our attention to extraordinary and rare things and impresses their significance on our minds (*Passions* II.75; CSM I, 355), Spinoza adopts a far less favorable stance on wonder, taking it to be an expression of ignorance, a condition which we seek to overcome (1app; G II.81).[32]

Having thinned out the primary passions to just three – joy, sadness, and desire – we are left to consider how they fit together and why they are all primary. The main problem here concerns how desire relates to the other two. While joy and sadness fit Spinoza's definition of affects, as increases and diminutions in one's power of acting, respectively (3p11s; defaff2–3), desire seems not to be a change in one's power of acting but a *response* to a change, a way in which one's striving is determined by an affection (defaff1).[33] And while emotions like joy and sadness, as representations of objects, have a mind-to-world direction of fit, desires seem to have a world-to-mind direction of fit, which is to say that they represent some condition that does not yet exist, seeking to make the world conform to this representation. While Spinoza may not be the only early modern philosopher to lump emotions and desires together under the rubric "affects,"[34] this might just reveal that he was not alone in his confusion.

Worse still, it is hard to see how these three affects could all be primary or nonderivative since desire appears to be at once more and less basic than the affects of joy and sadness. The view that desire is more basic than emotions is suggested by its conceptual ties to striving or appetite (3p9s). He claims that "desire is the very nature, *or* essence, of each [individual]" (3p57d), and that he recognizes no difference between desire and appetite, which is just one's striving expressed under the attributes of thought and extension (defaff1exp). If desire is one's striving or power of acting, and if joy and sadness are modifications of this striving, desire would be explanatorily prior to the other two affects.[35]

But we have also seen that Spinoza claims that desires are determined by how one is affected, or how one's essence is constituted, in which case one's desires are determined by one's emotions. Numerous passages suggest that emotions are explanatorily prior to desires, as when he writes: "The desire which *arises from* sadness or joy, and from hatred or love, is greater, the greater the affect is" (3p37).[36] If desire is parasitic on, and causally posterior to, forms of joy or sadness, it does not bear the marks of a primary affect.

Despite these grounds for thinking that there is some sort of priority relation between desire and emotion, we wish now to sketch a way of understanding how desire, joy, and sadness can all be understood as primary affects. With respect to the reasons for thinking that desire is prior to emotions, we must observe that it is a mistake to identify desire with striving *simpliciter*: striving is one's essence, while desire is an affect, or modification, of that essence. Spinoza is generally careful to flag that desire is a particular expression or modification of one's essence, as when he defines desire as "man's very essence, *insofar as it is conceived to be determined, from any given affection of it, to do something*" (defaff1, emphasis added). Of course, passages like this suggest that emotions are explanatorily prior to desires. But rather than understanding the "determination" relationship between desire and emotions to be one of causal priority, we propose that emotions and desire be understood as distinct aspects of one and the same essential constitution. Emotions give specific orientation to one's striving, and this specific orientation just *is* desire. So, while it might seem as though the formation of the emotion and the orientation of one's striving are successive moments in a process, in fact the orientation, i.e., the desire, is just the way in which forms of joy or sadness modify one's striving. While one can conceptually separate the emotion from the desire, emotions and particular desires are formed together.

A simple reflection on the general character of striving reveals why it would be a mistake to think of particular emotions and desires as distinct, successively formed modes. Since our striving, as our essence, must necessarily be expressed in all of our affections, it is not something that needs to be added to them. Rather there must be a conative side to any emotion, and this conative side is the desire. Emotions inform and direct our striving by registering changes in our power of acting and representing sources of this change.[37] When we consider the registration of these changes in isolation from the way they modify one's overall striving, we conceive of them as emotions. When we conceive of these changes against the backdrop of our overall striving, that is, as specific orientations of this striving, we conceive of them as desires. For instance, if I am enjoying lazing around in bed in the morning, this joy does not generate a distinct mental state that is the desire to stay in bed; the desire to stay in bed just is the motivational side of the joy itself. It is the form that my striving takes when I am affected with this particular kind of joy.

This conceptual distinction between emotion and desire may be illustrated in the following way. Imagine a trumpet through which wind is perpetually blowing. The ceaseless force of wind represents one's striving. If a valve is then pressed down, this act may be conceived in isolation from the sound produced, as a kind of structural change to the instrument. That would be equivalent to the emotion. However, we can also conceive of the depression of the valve in light of the wind being forced through trumpet, as a change in the sound produced. That would be equivalent to the desire – the way in which one's striving is constituted. The changing of the note (i.e., desire) just is what the pressing of the valve (i.e., emotion) does to the wind that is being forced through it. Desire is thus only conceptually distinct from emotions; emotion and desire are one and the same modification of one's striving, conceived in different ways. Consequently, desire, joy, and sadness can all be understood as primary (i.e., underived) affects.[38]

This account of desire as the conative aspect of emotions is quite remarkable. It implies that there is no gap whatsoever between one's affections and one's motivation – there is no moment of conative uptake during which one might resist one's emotional response. So, if one's emotional experience is not overtly expressed in one's striving, it can only be because a more powerful contrary emotional experience has overwhelmed it. How we are affected directly fixes how we strive: there is no further explanatory work to be done.

5.5 Passive and active affects

Spinoza also draws a distinction between two general categories of affect: those of which we are the adequate cause, and which arise only from adequate ideas, and those of which we are only a partial cause, or which arise from our interactions with other things and the confused representations that arise therefrom (3p3). The former are actions, or active affects, while the latter are passions, or passive affects. Because Spinoza describes passions in far more detail than he does active affects, and because the former comprise so much of our affective life, we will begin by discussing them.

Spinoza claims that passions of the mind are confused.[39] What accounts for this confusion? The most direct answer is that, as noted above, affects are complex modes of thought that are comprised of a representation of a change of one's power of acting and a representation of some putative cause. When it comes to the passions, the latter representation is a confused mode of imagination (gendefaff; G II, 204). So, when I take a sip of the coffee in my mug, I do not represent it distinctly, as it is in itself; rather, I represent the way that it affects and modifies my body (e.g., taste buds, neurotransmitters, etc.). And so my desire for coffee – which piggybacks on my perceptual representations of coffee – inherits this confusion.[40]

But capacity for passionate misrepresentation deepens due to associations. Ideas become associated when they arise at the same time (2p18) or resemble one another (3p16). Whole constellations of images and corresponding ideas are built on the basis of these associative relations, making it difficult to track with any precision what will actually bring joy or power. This may take relatively benign forms, as when listening to a record in a convivial environment leads one to overestimate the joy that the album will bring outside of that context, or when one desires the dark liquid denominated "coffee" at a convenience store, which, when consumed, brings more sadness than joy. But it can also take more noxious forms, as when a bad experience with one person leads one to fear or hate a whole class of individuals with whom one confusedly associates this individual (3p46). The affective valence transfers to things that bear no genuine connection to the actual source of joy or sadness.

Finally, passions also involve temporal and modal distortions. They lead us to prefer lesser, but temporally more proximate, joys to greater, but more distant, ones. And some passions are predicated on a false ascription of freedom to the proximate causes of our affects, as when one feels indignant towards another whom one regards as the sole cause of an insult or injury (defaff20). Such confused imputations of freedom only intensify the passion one feels (5p5, 5p5d, 3p49). If we were rational, however, we would pursue the greater good, irrespective of its temporal proximity, and we would regard all things as necessary (2p44).

In a variety of ways, then, passions are confused and unreliable representations. While they may lead us into empowering relationships, they often do not; and even when they do, they do so only accidentally and without security. They leave us adrift, striving on the basis of random personal encounters, idiosyncratic associations, and temporal and modal distortions (3p59s).[41]

Fortunately, while we are subjected to the passions, we are also capable of being guided by active affects. While other philosophers portray reason as fundamentally distinct from emotions and appetites, Spinoza rejects any sharp dichotomy between reason and emotions on the grounds that if they were independent, they could not causally interact. On his account, "[a]n affect cannot be restrained or taken away except by an affect opposite to, and stronger than, the affect to be restrained" (4p7). The adequate ideas of reason can restrain the passions because they are affective.

This raises the question of why there is an affective side – specifically a form of joy and a corresponding desire (3p59) – to adequate ideas. Spinoza's most direct explanation for this comes in 3p58d: "When the mind conceives itself and its power of acting, it rejoices (by p53). But the mind necessarily considers itself when it conceives a true, *or* adequate, idea (by 2p43). But the mind conceives some adequate ideas (by 2p40s2). Therefore, it also rejoices insofar as it conceives adequate ideas, i.e. (by p1), insofar as it acts" (3p58s). This account is somewhat limited in that it suggests that joy arises only from a reflective (second-order) idea of one's activity, rather than showing that there is an affective dimension to the first-order adequate idea. However, we think that Spinoza has the resources for defending the view that having first-order adequate ideas is itself joyful. To conceive of things adequately is to assert one's being or realize one's essence more fully. And to assert one's being, or realize one's essence, to a greater degree is to exhibit a greater power of acting. The affective side of this transition is, of course, joy. Simply put, to gain understanding is to increase one's (mental) power, and to increase one's power is to rejoice.[42]

The joy that accompanies adequate ideas orients one's striving, i.e., gives rise to desires. Spinoza claims that there are two general families of desire that arise insofar as one grasps things adequately: tenacity, or "the desire by which each one strives, solely from the dictate of reason, to preserve his being"; and nobility, or "the desire by which each one strives, solely from the dictate of reason, to aid other men and join them to him in friendship" (3p59s). The suggestion here is that there are actions and objects that we adequately conceive as empowering for us *and* there are actions and objects that we adequately conceive as empowering for others, and it is rational to desire both. But if "good" and "evil" are rooted in the striving to persevere in *one's own* being, it is hard to see what licenses Spinoza's commitment to the view that it is rational to pursue the empowerment of others. In the next chapter,[43] we will examine, and try to resolve, the tension between striving for oneself and striving for others.

5.6 Affects and sociality

Our discussion of Spinoza on the affects would be incomplete without a brief analysis of the social side of affective life. The linchpin here is Spinoza's account of the imitation of the affects, which gives rise to a range of harmonious and disharmonious consequences. The imitations of the affects states that: "If we imagine a thing like us, toward which we have had no affect, to be affected with some affect, we are thereby affected with a like affect" (3p27). The demonstration of this proposition reads:

> The images of things are affections of the human body whose ideas represent external bodies as present to us (by 2p17s), that is (by 2p16), whose ideas involve the nature of our body and at the same time the present nature of the external body. So if the nature of the external body is like the nature of our body, then the idea of the external body we imagine will involve an affection of our body like the affection of the external body. Consequently, if we imagine someone like us to be affected with some affect, this imagination will express an affection of our body like this affect. (3p27d)

There are a number of opaque claims here, but perhaps the central mystery is why representing an external body with a nature like one's own will result in one being affected in a similar way. One plausible explanation is that Spinoza's account of perception is modeled on a mechanistic account of the communication of motion: two bodies that are structurally similar will transmit motion in similar ways, and so will directly communicate motions to one another upon impact. Just as an inflamed body will set ablaze an adjacent body of a like nature, and a billiard ball will impart its motion upon striking another billiard ball, like beings will communicate affective states to one another.[44]

While, as an account of affective contagion, this is surely too crude, the basic phenomenon to which Spinoza is referring is widely accepted and well supported. Contemporary psychologists have noted that from a very early age, human children, and even other young primates, begin directly mimicking the facial expressions and affects of others.[45] In a particularly prescient passage, Spinoza seizes on the fact even small children imitate affects in support of his principle: "[W]e find from experience that children, because their bodies are continually, as it were, in a state of equilibrium, laugh or cry simply because they see others laugh or cry. Moreover, whatever they see others do, they immediately desire to imitate it" (3p32s).

The imitation of affects results in emulation, or "a desire for a thing which is generated in us because we imagine that others have the same desire" (defaff33, 3p27s), with emulation just being the conative side of imitation. And since affects and desires constitute evaluative judgments, it follows that, other things being equal, we love what others love, desire what others desire, and regard as good what others regard as good.

These considerations apply to our character or sense of self as much as to our actions: when we imagine that others approve of us, we feel self-esteem (3p30s, defaff25); when we imagine that others disapprove of us, we feel shame (3p30s, defaff31). For Spinoza, the desire for esteem plays an enormous role in our motivational economy, encouraging us to regulate our behavior to comport with cultural norms. And while shame itself, as a form of sadness and mark of impotence, is assuredly not a virtue, a "sense of shame" (defaff31exp) is generally preferable to its absence: "[S]hame, though not a virtue, is still good insofar as it indicates, in the man who blushes with shame, a desire to live honorably. [...] So though a man who is ashamed of some deed is really sad, he is still more perfect than one who is shameless, who has no desire to live honorably" (4p58s). Untouched by shame or concern for esteem, one would be relatively indifferent to many of the customs that help to unify a society (4p54s). We see from this how the imitation of affects can encourage social harmony, as it promotes affective and evaluative conformity along with a desire for esteem and an aversion to shame.

But the imitation of affects can also lead to conflict. For example, because affects constitute judgments, affective differences often manifest as evaluative disagreements. The imitation of affects entails that such outward disagreements come to be internalized, since when we are confronted by someone whose affective attitudes differs from ours, we undergo a "vacillation of mind" (3p17s), leaving us torn between contrary affects and judgments. This results in an unstable affective condition (5a1). And while Spinoza allows that such cognitive dissonance could be resolved by modifying one's own beliefs, he thinks that we are unlikely to do so because of another pervasive psychological trait: ambition.

Ambition is a protean concept for Spinoza. His first gloss of the term, as the "striving to do something (and also to omit doing something) solely to please men" (3p29s), seems harmless enough. However, just two propositions later, he construes ambition in a less benign way:

> This striving to bring it about that everyone should approve his love and hate is really ambition (see p29s). And so we see that each of us, by his nature, wants the others to live according to his judgment;

when all alike want this, they are alike an obstacle to one another, and when all wish to be praised, or loved, by all, they hate one another. (3p31s)

Because all ideas and ideational systems resist oppositional forces, we are averse to modifying our judgments. So, when disagreement erupts, we seek to diminish this dissonance by compelling others to judge in accordance with *our* judgments. And, of course, others are disposed to respond in the same way.

Ambition thus contributes to the persistence of disagreement, with disputants digging in their heels, redoubling their efforts at altering the other's judgments. When disagreements persist, dissonance is reduced only through hatred. Hatred overrides the imitation of affects (3p27d, 3p23), enabling one to retain one's viewpoint without much internal conflict.

The imitation of affects also facilitates another form of hatred, namely, envy, which Spinoza defines as "hate insofar as it so affects a man that he is saddened by another's happiness and, conversely, glad at his ill fortune" (defaff33).[46] Envy arises when someone else enjoys something desirable that only one person can possess (3p32). By enabling one to participate, to some degree, in the joy of others, the imitation of affects can heighten one's sense of deprivation, stoking further envy and resentment. So, if a coworker gets a promotion for which I was also a candidate, I will not only share in her joy to some degree, I will also experience this as a joy which I was denied, which will lead me to feel envious. This helps to explain Spinoza's claim that "from the same property of human nature from which it follows that men are compassionate," namely, the imitation of affects, "it also follows that the same men are envious and ambitious" (3p32s).

But while the imitation of affects can breed such antisocial consequences, we are not condemned to a life of internal and external conflict. Spinoza advances ethical and political remedies to hatred and intolerance. We will explore these successively in the next two chapters.

Further reading

Carriero, John. 2005. "Spinoza on Final Causality," in Daniel Garber and Steven Nadler (eds), *Oxford Studies in Early Modern Philosophy*, Vol. II, pp. 105–47. Oxford: Clarendon Press.

Garrett, Don. 2018. *Nature and Necessity in Spinoza's Philosophy*. Oxford: Oxford University Press, chs 11–13.

James, Susan. 1997. *Passion and Action: The Emotions in Seventeenth-Century Philosophy*. Oxford: Clarendon Press.

Jaquet, Chantal. 2018. *Affects, Actions and Passions in Spinoza: The Unity of Body and Mind*, trans. Tatiana Reznichenko. Edinburgh: Edinburgh University Press.

Steinberg, Justin. 2016. "Affect, Desire, and Judgement in Spinoza's Account of Motivation." *British Journal for the History of Philosophy* 24(1): 67–87.

Viljanen, Valtteri. 2011. *Spinoza's Geometry of Power*. Cambridge: Cambridge University Press, chs 4–6.

Yovel, Yirmiyahu (ed.). 1999. *Desire and Affect: Spinoza as Psychologist*. New York: Little Room Press.

6

Moral Philosophy

Many first-time readers can be forgiven for being somewhat puzzled by the title of Spinoza's masterwork. Spinoza is typically first encountered in a survey course, where the focus will likely be on how Spinoza's metaphysics – e.g., his monism and treatment of the mind–body relationship – differs from Descartes. But while Spinoza's metaphysics is very rich and interesting on its own, this approach regrettably leaves out the very point of the work, which is to articulate a conception of moral development or liberation within the confines of a naturalistic metaphysics.

Even those who make it to the latter half of the work might worry that Spinoza is committed to theses that preclude the possibility of an ethics. The ontological and modal status of human beings seems to render us unfit for moral agency. It is not clear how humans, as modes or affections of substance, rather than as substances, can also be centers of activity, especially since we are also *necessitated*, lacking the free will that is widely assumed to be a precondition of moral agency. Moreover, Spinoza himself flatly asserts that "[a]s far as good and evil are concerned, they [...] indicate nothing positive in things, considered in themselves" (4pref). So, in addition to holding metaphysical positions that seem to leave little space for human agency, Spinoza also directly expresses views that seem to relegate morality to the confused and illusory domain of the imagination. The aim of this chapter will be to explain how Spinoza develops an ethics of empowerment or liberation within the confines of his naturalistic metaphysics, showing how he overcomes the challenges noted above.

6.1 The critique of intrinsic normativity

After establishing that there is just one substance, God or Nature, and that everything follows from the necessity of God's nature, Spinoza turns in the appendix to *Ethics* part 1 to account for the pervasive and persistent prejudice that Nature acts with human welfare in view, to expose the falsity of this position, and to debunk confusions that arise out of it. Specifically, he aims to undermine belief in what we have called intrinsic normativity, or the view that evaluative predicates like good, evil, beautiful, ugly, perfect, and imperfect refer to intrinsic properties of things. He writes:

> After men persuaded themselves that everything which happens, happens on their account, they had to judge that what is most important in each thing is what is most useful to them, and to rate as most excellent all those things by which they were most pleased. Hence, they had to form these notions, by which they explained natural things: *good, evil, order, confusion, warm, cold, beauty, ugliness.* And because they think themselves free, those notions have arisen: *praise* and *blame, sin* and *merit.* (1app; G II, 81)

The anthropocentrism that underlies the belief that God acts, as humans do, with an end in view – specifically, that "God has made all things for man" – leads people to suppose further that things that happen in nature are intrinsically good or evil, beautiful or ugly, and so forth. As we have seen, this is rooted in a wholly mistaken conception of God.[1] Spinoza takes great pains to deny intrinsic normativity, claiming that the belief that good, evil, and so forth are intrinsic features of the world arises only when we confuse the imagination with the intellect. In other words, we take notions that are mere "modes of imagining," reflecting our subjective, embodied experience of things, and treat them as though they were genuine properties of nature (G II, 82–3). Specifically, people call things "good or evil, sound or rotten and corrupt as they are affected by it" (1app; G II, 82), treating our own, potentially idiosyncratic experiences of things as if they were features of the things themselves.

Spinoza's critique of intrinsic normativity here resembles, and may well have been inspired by, Hobbes. In *Leviathan*, Hobbes maintains that evaluative judgments denote a condition of the perceiver rather than a property of the object itself:

> But whatsoever is the object of any man's appetite or desire; that is it, which he for his part calleth *good*: and the object of his hate, and

aversion, *evil*; and of his contempt, *vile* and *inconsiderable*. For these words of good, evil, and contemptible, are ever used with relation to the person that useth them: there being nothing simply and absolutely so[.] (*Leviathan* I.6; EW III.41)

For Hobbes, appetites and aversions are highly variable, reflecting the diversity of people's bodily constitutions; so it can hardly be expected that "*all men consent, in the desire of almost any one and the same object*" (*Leviathan* I.6; EW III.41). Like Hobbes, Spinoza thinks that because each person "judge[s] things according to the disposition of his brain," evaluative conflicts are inevitable: "For although human bodies agree in many things, they still differ in very many. And for that reason what seems good to one, seems bad to another" (1app; G II, 82–3). By debunking the notion of intrinsic normativity, Spinoza hopes to defuse a great many pointless controversies.

Spinoza resumes his critique of the view that normative concepts refer to real features of things in themselves in the preface to *Ethics* part 4, where the discussion focuses on the concepts of perfection and imperfection. Here Spinoza once again claims that behind the ordinary use of these concepts is the noxious prejudice that Nature acts with a purpose – as if there were ideals or models for how things ought to be and that Nature has failed or sinned when something comes into existence that falls short of these models. Spinoza, of course, rejects the view that in addition to the necessary order of Nature, there is also a normative order of Nature – a way that things ought to be that is distinct from the way things are.[2] The models or standards by which we judge things to be perfect or imperfect are not inscribed in Nature itself; rather, they are human constructs that arise because we form universal ideas of things and come to "prefer some models to others" (4pref; G II, 206). For instance, what counts as a perfect romantic partner or a perfect vacation will differ from individual to individual, according to the preferences from which people construct their models.

Once again, we see that evaluative concepts do not refer to intrinsic features of the world but are fundamentally *desire-relative*. This point is reinforced when Spinoza turns once again to "good" and "evil" later in the same preface, which is where he baldly states that they are not features of things "in themselves": if a thing agrees more with the ends or models that we set based on our desires, we call it good; if a thing clashes with these ends or models, we call it evil. These passages give the impression that Spinoza aims not so much to advance an ethics as to debunk all ethics, exposing moral reasoning to consist in nothing more than expressions of subjective tastes and preferences. Ideas of good and evil are mere confused projections of the imagination,[3] and if one were perfectly rational, one would have no knowledge of good and evil (4p68). One can see from these claims why Nietzsche would declare in an 1881 letter to Franz Overbeck that upon reading Spinoza he had discovered a precursor (*Vorgänger*), another critic of ordinary morality and religion.

6.2 Grounding goodness

Still, Spinoza does not wish to jettison the concepts of good, evil, perfection, and imperfection altogether. Indeed, he insists that "we must retain these words" (4pref; G II, 208), offering revisionary, well-grounded versions of these concepts in place of confused and baseless alternatives. At the root of his account of normative concepts is, unsurprisingly, the doctrine of striving. Complex individuals, like human beings, are highly composite things that possess a certain form or patterned communication between constituent parts.[4] So, as modes, we are not *mere* properties; we are also things with an essential structure and integrity. As unified complex things, we strive to persevere in our being – that is, to maintain the integrity of our body and to increase our power of acting – as far as possible. And, while "good" and "evil" are not properties of things in themselves, there is a standard by which we may rightly judge things to be good or evil, namely in terms of the extent to which they serve to aid or obstruct our essential and ineliminable striving. Spinoza advances several constructive accounts of good and evil, which, as we will see, are coextensive. Consider the following definitions:

> By good I shall understand what we certainly know to be useful to us. (4def1)

> By evil, however, I shall understand what we certainly know prevents us from being masters of some good. (4def2)

It is not entirely clear why Spinoza restricts "good" and "evil" to what we "certainly know" to be useful or to be an obstacle to utility, but perhaps this qualification is intended to rule out things that are only accidentally, and not essentially, useful – things that we could not certainly know to be useful. A more pressing question is what exactly Spinoza means by "useful" here. The answer becomes clear in the demonstration to 4p8:

> We call good, or evil, what is useful to, or harmful to, preserving our being (by def1 and def2), that is (by 3p7), what increases or diminishes, aids or restrains, our power of acting. Therefore (by the definitions of joy and sadness in 3p11s), insofar as we perceive that a thing affects us with joy or sadness, we call it good or evil. (4p8d)

The first sentence of this quote clarifies that "usefulness" is to be understood in terms of promoting our striving or increasing our power of acting. The second sentence reminds us that increases in power are experienced affectively as joy, while decreases in power are experienced as sadness. Consequently, things are good to the extent and only to the extent that they lead to joy. This fits with Spinoza's earlier assertion that by good he understands "every kind of joy, and whatever leads to it" (3p39s).

There is one final formulation that looks rather different from the others. It comes immediately after Spinoza has criticized our tendency to judge things to be perfect or imperfect (good or evil) in relation to arbitrary models. Here he claims that "because we desire to form an idea of man, as a model of human nature which we may look to, it will be useful to us to retain these same words with the meaning I have indicated" (4pref; G II, 208). This *model of human nature* then serves as the standard against which we may make normative judgments:

> In what follows, therefore, I shall understand by good what we know certainly is a means by which we may approach nearer and nearer to the model of human nature we set before ourselves. By evil, what we certainly know prevents us from becoming like that model. Next, we shall say that men are more perfect or imperfect, insofar as they approach more or less near to this model. (4pref; G II, 208)

This passage raises a couple of questions. First, how does this formulation of "good" as that which we know brings us closer to the model of human nature relate to the other formulations? Second, given that Spinoza spends much of the preface criticizing the normative judgments people make based on their own idiosyncratic models, what makes his model of human nature a less dubious touchstone?

In terms of the question of compatibility, there is a quite tidy way of connecting this formulation to the others: the model of human nature that he is describing here is a model of a maximally powerful human being. This model arises out of our essential striving for power as a kind of projection of this desire. Spinoza already suggests something like this in an earlier work: "[M]eanwhile man conceives a human nature much stronger and more enduring than his own, and at the same time sees that nothing prevents his acquiring such a nature, [so] he is spurred to seek means that will lead him to such a perfection. Whatever can be a means to his attaining it is called a true good" (TIE, §13).

If the model that we adopt as the standard is just a paradigm of human power, then all of the formulations that Spinoza advances for conceiving of goodness are in fact interchangeable: *things are good for us to the extent and only to the extent that they are useful*, or *increase our power of acting*, or *bring us joy*, or *bring us closer to the model of human nature*.

As for the second question, what distinguishes Spinoza's model from those deployed in confused judgments of good and evil is that his is strictly indexed to our essential, ineliminable striving for power. Whereas normative judgments and the models on which they depend typically reflect haphazard experiences and associations, making normative judgments highly idiosyncratic and confused, Spinoza seeks to ground the standard of goodness in our constitutive motivational tendency, out of which all particular desires spring. Indeed, as Spinoza sees it, all particular desires are specifications of this primordial striving, channeling this striving in particular ways, some of which (active desires) direct us to do things that are reliably conducive to our power, others of which (passions) direct us in ways that are likely to undermine this very power. Unlike the arbitrary models that spring from confused passions, Spinoza's model of human nature is a crystallized vision of our real interests, a conception of what we would want if we were fully rational.

Spinoza's revisionary account of normativity also differs from the accounts that he criticizes in that he has thoroughly dispelled the illusion that good and evil are intrinsic properties of things. He presents us instead with a conception of ethics as thoroughly motivation-relative, rooted in the striving of a particular thing. Rather than regarding things as good or evil in themselves, we are presented with an alternative according to which things are good or evil based on how they affect some particular striving thing. Consequently, "one and the same thing can, at the same time, be good, and bad, and also indifferent. For example, music is good for one who is melancholy, bad for one who is mourning, and neither good nor bad to one who is deaf" (4pref; G II, 208). Good and evil are always tied to a perspective.

In certain respects, then, "good" and "evil" are similar to so-called secondary qualities, or response-dependent features of things, like warm, cold, bitter, sweet, and so on. When I call water warm, I might *seem* to be reporting an intrinsic feature of water; but, in fact, I am reporting how *I* experience – or would experience under normal observation conditions – the mean kinetic activity of the water molecules. Likewise, when I call something good, I project this quality onto things as if it were in them itself; but, in fact, I am simply reporting how I am affected by these things. Spinoza himself suggests a connection between normative concepts and secondary qualities when he groups "warm" and "cold" alongside "good" and "evil" in his list of notions that are mere modes of imagining that we often project onto the world (1app; G II, 81).

But even if normative concepts and secondary qualities are both, in some sense, response dependent, there are important differences between them. For instance, when it comes to secondary qualities, often one's perception or response is authoritative. If a dish tastes salty or bitter to you, it is salty or bitter *by your tastes*. One can try to adjust for features of the observation conditions that might affect one's experience, as when being on a particular medication makes everything taste bitter; but bitterness itself is ultimately a subjective taste experience. For Spinoza, ethics is not response dependent in this way. Good and evil are rooted in how something *really* affects one's striving for power, irrespective of one's subjective experience. Water *really is* good for the person who is dehydrated, even if she does not feel thirsty; and it is bad for the person with dropsy, no matter how much she craves it.[5] Now, since increases of power are experienced as joy and decreases are experienced as sadness, one's experience will to some degree track the objective impact of a thing on one's striving. But, as we will explore in more depth now, one's subjective, affective attitude towards a thing can profoundly come apart from its actual impact on one's power of acting. Whether or not a thing *actually* is good for one is not determined by one's perception of it.

6.3 Bondage to the passions

As noted in the introductory chapter,[6] Spinoza famously opens his early *Treatise on the Emendation of the Intellect* with a stylized autobiographical account of his pursuit of a "true good" or a lasting source of joy (TIE, §1). He identifies three particular things that people pursue as ultimate ends, but which fail to provide enduring satisfaction: wealth, honor, and sensual pleasure. These pursuits simply distract and dull the mind, while begetting unsatisfiable desires (TIE, §§4–6). This leads Spinoza to conclude that "all those things men ordinarily strive for, not only provide no remedy to preserve our being, but in fact hinder that preservation" (TIE, §7). This raises a general question for Spinoza's philosophy: if affects register changes in our power such that when our power is increased we experience joy, and if we desire things that cause us joy, how do we come to desire destructive things?

Part of the reason why we pursue destructive things is that when we are guided by the passions, we confusedly represent the objects of desire. To see why the imagination gives rise to destructive desires, we must recall some of the sources of confusion.[7] When one represents something via the imagination, one represents its object in a fragmentary and mutilated way. So, when one perceives the sun, one represents it only insofar as it affects one's body; such a representation reveals more about the state of one's own body than it does about the sun itself (2p16c2). This confusion is compounded by haphazard and idiosyncratic associations. If distinct things strike one as bearing a likeness to one another, the imagination will run them together (3p16d), forming an idea that is too indeterminate to pick out any precise referent. Consequently, even if elm trees affect me differently from oak trees – say, if I am highly allergic to elm trees but not to oaks – I might not represent them distinctly. We can see how the formation of confused, indeterminate ideas can contribute to misdirected striving since even if I do not have a reason to avoid oak trees in bloom, my confused ideas might lead me to respond as if I do.

In addition to resemblance, ideas also get associated with one another when two things are temporally connected through one's experiences (2p18). So, for example, if Mary experiences the first pangs of appendicitis while at a local bakery, she is likely to be reminded of this pain when she thinks of this bakery. And her affective responses will become confused through this very association: the suffering from the pain will affect the way that she thinks about the bakery, experiencing a tinge of distress when she thinks about it. This leads Spinoza to claim that "[a]ny thing can be the accidental cause of joy, sadness, or desire" (3p15) since anything can come to be arbitrarily associated with things that actually do bring joy or sadness. Put simply, we judge objects in ways that are too coarse-grained to track their value in relation to our power of acting. So part of the explanation for how our striving gets misdirected has to do with confused representations of things.

Another part of the explanation is that the *intensity* of passions often fails to track the overall and long-term impact of the objects that are represented. With respect to the question of whether a thing is good vis-à-vis some thing's striving, we must look to its *overall* impact. If a thing gives rise to a form of joy, we must ask further whether it increases the power of the *whole* person or just some *parts* of the person, and whether this increase is enduring or short-lived. With respect to the question of parts and wholes, Spinoza draws an important distinction between *cheerfulness* (*hilaritas*), a form of joy that affects the whole person, and *pleasure* (*titillatio*), a form of joy that affects one part of the person more than the rest (3p11s). Eating a donut might be more pleasant than reading Walt Whitman, and so might prompt a more intense desire, even if reading Whitman promises a more pervasive increase in one's power. Whereas cheerfulness is good for the whole person, pleasure can actually interfere with one's general flourishing (4p43).

The difference between cheerfulness and pleasure also plays out over time. Cheerfulness is always good (4p48), leaving only joy in its wake. However, forms of pleasure are often followed by sadness and regret. Here we may recall Spinoza's observation that the pursuit of sensual pleasure, wealth, and honor dull the mind,[8] diminishing one's long-term power, even if acquiring these goods brings a temporary affective boost. And, with respect to sensual pleasure, "after the enjoyment of sensual pleasure is past, the greatest sadness follows" (TIE, §4). This exposes the limitations of pleasure: by exciting one part of the mind, it often stultifies the rest and gives way to long-term sadness.

So, when we are in the grips of the passions, we not only represent the objects of desire confusedly, pursuing things that are not really the source of joy and avoiding things that are, we are also led by forms of pleasure that are disempowering on the whole and in the long term. Spinoza thus concludes his analysis of the passions in *Ethics* part 3 by claiming that they leave us adrift, "like waves on the sea, driven by contrary winds, we toss about, not knowing our outcome and fate" (3p59s), failing to descry and pursue sources of enduring joy and power.

The image of wayward striving with which Spinoza concludes *Ethics* part 3 differs somewhat from the conception of unfreedom with which he opens *Ethics* part 4. The former seems to depict the "slave" (*servum*), whom Spinoza describes in the *Ethics* as one who "does those things *he is most ignorant of*" (4p66s, emphasis added) and in the TTP as one "who is drawn by his own pleasure, and *can neither see nor do* anything useful to himself" (TTP 16.32; G III, 194, emphasis added). The full-fledged slave strives blindly, in ignorance. By contrast, one who is in the condition of bondage described in the preface of *Ethics* part 4 "sees the better for himself," even if he is still "forced to follow the worse." Unlike the blind servitude of the preceding passages, this form of bondage – often characterized as a form of *akrasia* or incontinence – involves a distinct form of internal conflict or dissonance. As Spinoza puts it in 4p17s, "the true knowledge of good and evil arouses disturbances of the mind," citing as support a passage from *Ecclesiastes*: "He who increases knowledge increases sorrow." Spinoza likely opts to focus on this form of bondage because it affects even those who are partially rational, even those readers who have come to acknowledge the futility and excesses of many passionate desires. He regards coming to understand the reasons why we struggle with, and often fall prey to, the passions as an essential step on the path to liberty: "[I]t is necessary to come to know both our nature's power *and its lack of power*, so that we can determine what reason can do in moderating the affects, and what it cannot do" (4p17s, emphasis added).

There are several key claims in his explanation for why we remain susceptible to this form of bondage. The first is that we are inescapably passive, to some degree. This is a simple by-product of the fact that we are a "part of Nature, which cannot be conceived through itself, without others" (4p2), that we never overcome this condition (4p4), and that our power is surpassed by the power of other things that can limit our striving (4p3, 4a1).

This establishes that "man is necessarily always subject to passions" (4p4c), but it does not yet explain how it happens that we are led by the passions *even when we know better*. For this, we need a second thesis, namely that affects can only be restrained by stronger affects (4p7). This reflects Spinoza's rejection of the reason–emotion dichotomy. If reason were entirely distinct from the emotions, it could not restrain them. However, as we have seen, Spinoza thinks that in addition to the passions, there are active or rational affects, which are forms of joy that we experience insofar as we understand things (3p58).[9] Consequently, reason *can* restrain the power of sad passions, but only insofar as rational joy is more powerful than the passions. And Spinoza insists that the mere fact that an idea is true does not ensure superior affective power: "[I]maginations do not disappear through the presence of the true insofar as it is true, but because there occur others, *stronger than them*, which *exclude the present existence* of the things we imagine" (4p1s, emphases added).

To appreciate Spinoza's point here, consider for instance the fear of plane travel. For someone in the grip of this fear, the facts about the relative safety of plane travel are not likely to allay the anxiety in any significant way: the confused fear is more potent than one's knowledge of the facts. The same is true for any phobia. One cannot dispel phobias through the accumulation of more true ideas alone; one must rather find ways to make the true ideas more powerful or vivid, or to attenuate the power of the passions themselves (say, through exposure therapy). The crucial insight here is that it is an idea's potency, not its truth-value, that determines the extent to which it directs the mind.

In the middle of this analysis of why we sometimes act contrary to what we know to be better, Spinoza advances his bold and interesting claim about the nature of evaluative judgments,[10] according to which evaluative judgments about particular objects (i.e., *this thing* is good or bad) are constituted by one's affective attitude in relation to that object: judging something to be good or evil is nothing more than representing that thing affectively. The value that the greedy man puts on money is expressed by his greed itself (3p39s). The evaluation is constituted by the affect. In grounding evaluative judgments in affects, Spinoza is not claiming, as David Hume later would, that reason is necessarily a slave to the passions since, once again, reason is *itself* affective. The significance of this account of evaluative judgment for Spinoza's account of *akrasia* is that it allows him to argue that (1) even rational or accurate evaluative judgments are themselves affects, and (2) as such they can be overpowered by other affects. He proceeds to make the second claim explicit in 4p15, relying on the thesis that desires are just the conative side of affects: "A desire which arises from a true knowledge of good and evil can be extinguished or restrained by many other desires which arise from affects by which we are tormented."

The final step of Spinoza's analysis of akratic bondage is his account of why irrational passions often overwhelm rational desires.

In 4p9–p12, Spinoza shows that the intensity of an affect varies according to temporal proximity and the represented modality. Simply put, affects that are directed towards present, temporally proximate, or necessary things will be more intense than affects directed at temporally distant or contingent things. He then proceeds to argue that since passionate desires can overwhelm rational desires in general (4p15), this is all the more common when rational desires are directed at future or contingent things, while passionate desires are directed at present goods (4p16–p17).[11] While to the extent that people conceive of things rationally, they will be "affected equally, whether the idea is of a future or past thing, or of a present one" (4p62), in fact our assessments typically reflect the distorting influence of the passions, leading us to prefer lesser, but temporally more proximate, forms of pleasure to greater, but more distant, forms of joy. So, even when we "see the better" – for instance, when we recognize that we will be happier and healthier if we get some exercise – this recognition *qua* affect can be easily overcome by the present aversion to physical discomfort.

On the basis of this analysis, Spinoza concludes: "With these few words I have explained the causes of man's lack of power and inconstancy, and why men do not observe the precepts of reason" (4p18s). We strive waywardly not only when we fail to recognize our true good – when we make confused judgments about what will bring us lasting joy or power – but also when we recognize our true good, provided that this recognition is not sufficiently affectively intense to overwhelm the passions. This reveals something really significant about Spinoza's ethical project: in order to become more rational, it is not enough to apprehend things correctly; this true apprehension must be imbued with sufficient affective strength to restrain one's confused ideas or passions. So, while Spinoza's moral philosophy may be construed as intellectualist insofar as its aim is to emend or correct one's beliefs, it is equally true that it is sentimentalist, insofar as it is the affective power of these ideas that determines the extent to which those ideas govern our minds.

6.4 Human freedom

Having analyzed Spinoza's views on bondage, we may now turn to his views about human freedom. If one thinks that in order to be free one must possess a faculty of will that is not determined by causes, then one will not find a satisfactory account of agency in Spinoza.

However, there are reasons to think that having an absolutely free or uncaused will is actually incompatible with human agency since in order to exercise agential control, one's actions must be explicable in terms of a cause or reason for one's action. If one were to act from an uncaused will, there would be an explanatory gap between the reasons that one has for acting and one's behavior. To see why such explanatory gaps would be a problem for agency, consider the following example: a friend invites you to go with her to a concert, you really like the artist, you are offered the ticket for free, and you have no other obligations that night. In short, the reasons all clearly line up in favor of going to the concert. So you go to the concert. The question is whether the reasons *sufficiently explain* why you attend the concert. If they do, then there is no further explanatory work to be done by a faculty of "will": the reasons fully explain your behavior, which enables one to attribute the action to you. But if the reasons do not sufficiently explain the behavior, we are left either to conclude that the behavior was random, and so not under one's control, or we must fill the gap by appealing to something *other* than your reasons. But what could this something else be, and how would it help to preserve agency? We might want to appeal to the will here, but then we must ask why you willed what you did? If we appeal to reasons, then it looks once again like reasons are doing all of the explanatory work. If, however, the will is not guided by reasons, then once again it looks like the effects are random and so cannot properly be attributed to the agent. The activity of a will would no more be under an agent's control than an epileptic convulsion is. It may well be, then, that having an absolutely unconstrained will is incompatible with agential control.[12]

On Spinoza's view, freedom consists not in the absence of causation but in the right kind of causation. We see something like this expressed in a 1674 letter to Hugo Boxel, where he denies that "necessary" and "free" are contraries, accusing Boxel of failing to distinguish between constraint or force, and necessity (Ep. 56). It is *constraint*, not necessity, that is opposed to freedom. The distinction between things that are free and things that are constrained turns on the source of the necessity: to the extent that a thing brings about effects from its own nature, the thing is free; but to the extent that the effects depend on external causes, the thing is constrained. This is consistent with how Spinoza defines freedom at the beginning of the *Ethics*: "That thing is said to be free which exists solely from the necessity of its own nature, and is determined to action by itself alone" (1def7). Only God is completely free in this sense since only God acts entirely from its own nature. As noted above, human beings are always to some extent passive, constrained by other things. Nevertheless, humans can exercise a certain *degree* of freedom: we are free to the extent that we are able to exist and act from our nature alone.[13] The more active, or causally powerful, we are, the freer we are.

The emphasis on causal power runs throughout Spinoza's moral philosophy. We have already seen, for instance, that Spinoza understands "good" and "evil" in terms of how a thing affects one's power of acting. The same applies to "virtue."[14] While there is a strong precedent for thinking of virtue, *virtus* in Latin, in terms of a kind of aptitude or power connected to one's flourishing, Spinoza pushes this connection to the extreme, treating virtue as identical with causal power: the more powerful one is, the more virtuous one is. This highlights once again the way that Spinoza grounds normativity in one's striving. We cannot exhibit any other virtue or conceive of anything as valuable or desirable without this essential striving to exist and act. And while all things strive for power, not all things strive effectively. It is only those who are successful at striving that can be said to be virtuous: "The more each one strives, *and is able*, to seek his own advantage, that is to preserve his being, the more he is endowed with virtue" (4p20, emphasis added). In the language of contemporary ethics, Spinoza seems to be advancing a desire-satisfaction theory of both morality and happiness. In this respect, Spinoza's moral philosophy seems to align nicely with Hobbes's. In *Leviathan*, Hobbes defines "felicity" as *"continual success* in obtaining those things which a man from time to time desireth" (*Leviathan* I.6; EW III, 51). Bearing in mind that for Spinoza our essential and ineliminable appetite is to persevere in our being, Spinoza seems to echo Hobbes when he writes: "[H]appiness consists in a man's being able to preserve his being" (4p18s).[15]

But despite this surface-level resemblance, Spinoza's view diverges from Hobbes in a crucial respect. Whereas Hobbes treats all desires that arise out of one's striving or endeavor as equal, taking happiness to consist in the satisfaction of *whatever* desires one happens to have, Spinoza, as we have seen, sharply distinguishes between desires that arise out of inadequate ideas and desires that arise out of adequate ideas. Only insofar as we are guided by adequate ideas can we be said to act from virtue or one's striving alone, as opposed to being pushed around by external causes: "A man cannot be said absolutely to act from virtue insofar as he is determined to do something because he has inadequate ideas, but only insofar as he is determined because he understands" (4p23). The demonstration to this proposition makes it clear that he takes acting from virtue to consist in acting from adequate ideas (from 3p1), or acting in the strict sense. Virtuous striving is rational striving because, for Spinoza, knowledge is power.

At this point, though, we should pause on this formulation, which masks an ambiguity that goes to the heart of our understanding of Spinoza's moral philosophy. One way of understanding the claim that knowledge is power is to take knowledge to be an enabling capacity: it allows us to discern what is valuable and to take appropriate steps to acquire those things. Francis Bacon advanced an unabashedly instrumentalist version of the thesis that knowledge is power. According to him, knowledge enables us to achieve insights and forge new tools that afford us more control over nature. Hobbes too includes "knowledge" (*scientia*) among the powers of man and describes the laws of nature as precepts or rules of reason that enable us to preserve ourselves (*Leviathan* I.10, I.14; EW III, 75, 116–17). Reason is an *instrument* to power or preservation. It is natural to take what Spinoza calls "dictates of reason" to be like Hobbesian laws of nature: rules for striving effectively or enhancing one's power.[16]

However, there is another way of understanding the view that knowledge is power, which is that knowledge is *intrinsically* empowering. The more one understands things, the more powerful one is *in virtue of that very act of understanding*. Spinoza evidently thinks that adequately understanding things is itself empowering and joyful (3p58), and much of what he describes concerning the role of reason looks like statements about which kinds of affects follow from reason and which do not – in other words, they look less like rules for action than descriptions of what rational life is like.[17] Furthermore, Spinoza seems to indicate that he is not especially concerned with the performance or non-performance of particular actions, writing that "no action, considered in itself, is good or evil" (4p59d2). Thrashing one's arms up and down might be an expression of anger but it might also be a joyful expression of one's physical capacities, as in a dance.[18] Passages like this suggest that Spinoza conceives of virtue or rational striving primarily in terms of clarifying one's understanding, or getting one's mind right, rather than figuring out how best to achieve some *further* goal. Striving for power may thus be conceptualized as a striving for knowledge (4p26–p28) since knowledge is intrinsically and directly empowering.

In fact, Spinoza accepts both of these ways of conceiving of knowledge as power. Knowledge is both intrinsically empowering and a tool for further power. Correspondingly, Spinoza's *Ethics* is at once a cognitive therapy and a guide to practical action that concerns how we engage, and enter into communities, with one another. We will take these in turn, beginning with the latter.

Altruism and sociality

Given Spinoza's insistence that "the foundation of virtue is this very striving to preserve one's own being" (4p18s), it is tempting to regard Spinoza's ethical philosophy as a form of egoism, as the good consists in something like enlightened self-interest. However, if we read further in that same scholium, we find remarks that problematize a simple egoistic reading:

> Of [those things outside of us which are useful], we can think of none more excellent than those which agree entirely with our nature. For if, for example, two individuals of entirely the same nature are joined to one another, they compose an individual twice as powerful as each one. To man, then, there is nothing more useful than man. Man, I say, can wish for nothing more helpful to the preservation of his being than that all should so agree in all things that the minds and bodies of all would compose, as it were, one mind and one body; that all should strive together, as far as they can, to preserve their being; and that all, together, should seek for themselves the common advantage of all.
>
> From this it follows that men who are governed by reason – i.e., men who, from the guidance of reason, seek their own advantage – want nothing for themselves that they do not desire for other men. Hence, they are just, honest, and honorable. (4p18s)[19]

But why does Spinoza think it is rational to desire for others what one desires for oneself?

The simple answer is that to the extent that we can join with other humans who agree with us in nature, we are empowered. Spinoza argues for this position in the middle propositions of *Ethics* part 4. In 4p31, he writes that "[i]nsofar as a thing agrees with our nature, it is necessarily good." He defends this by invoking the conatus doctrine, from which he concludes that things that agree in nature cannot destroy each other (4p30d) and must in fact aid in the preservation of this common nature (4p31c). However, Spinoza certainly does not think that human beings are always helpful towards one another, for insofar as we are guided by passions, we do not agree in nature and can be drawn into conflicts (4p32–p34). Rather, he claims that "[o]nly insofar as men live according to the guidance of reason, must they always agree in nature" (4p35). The main idea here is that only insofar as we are rational do we act in ways that are explicable "through human nature alone," rather than being impelled by external causes (4p35d). Insofar as people are rational, and so agree in their human nature, they aid one another. As he puts it: "There is no singular thing in Nature which is more useful to man than a man who lives according to the guidance of reason. [...] [M]an is a God to man" (4p35c1–p35s). We desire for others what we desire for ourselves (4p37), namely, knowledge (4p26), which theoretically "can be possessed equally by all men" (4p36d) since knowledge acquisition is not a zero-sum game. Indeed, the more knowledgeable others are, the more one's own striving for knowledge will be encouraged and aided (4p37d2). The upshot of all of this is that Spinoza thinks that to the extent that we are rational, we will seek the good of others just as we seek our own good. By insisting that one who is rational pursues the good of all humans (4p35d), and by denying that self-interest conflicts with altruism (4p35c2), Spinoza further distances himself from the more individualistic Hobbesian approach to ethics.

But even if Spinoza maintains that rational humans will act in ways that are beneficial to one another, one might raise questions about whether he is entitled to such a position. Specifically, his arguments for altruism seem to hinge on the belief that there is a shared human nature, which is at odds with apparent expressions of nominalism, as when he refers to "man" as a confused universal (2p40s1). Moreover, even if people do share a nature in some sense, it seems evident that another's particular striving is numerically distinct from one's own; so it is hard to see how aiding another's striving is *by that very fact* aiding one's own striving.

These are difficult interpretative matters that cannot be definitively settled here. However, we will consider some potential responses. With respect to the question of whether Spinoza's commitment to a common "human nature" conflicts with his denial of universals like "human," it is quite likely that Spinoza thinks that the natures of individual human beings have enough in common with one another – the structures of our bodies and minds are sufficiently alike – that we can, for the sake of convenience, talk as if there is a single human nature, even if strictly speaking all essences are unique.[20] As for the further problem of why we desire the good for others whose natures are similar to ours, one explanation is simply that helping others become more rational is beneficial to oneself: it renders others less socially destructive, enables one to enter into more productive relationships and more complete unions with them, and indirectly helps to strengthen one's own resolve in pursuit of knowledge (4p37d2, 4p40, 4app).[21] Consequently, doing what is good for others or one's community is a way of pursuing one's own good.

While Spinoza's conception of morality resembles traditional conceptions in stressing the importance of aiding others, in other respects it appears less conventional. For instance, the way that he distances himself from religious – especially Christian – ethics forms the most striking part of his moral philosophy. While he embraces Christian teaching of returning hate with love (4p46), he denies that Christian virtues like pity (4p50), humility (4p53), and repentance (4p54) are good in themselves, promoting cheerfulness and proper self-esteem in their place. One can imagine Nietzsche reading this stretch of the *Ethics* with enthusiastic approval. Still, in denying that pity, humility, and repentance are good in themselves, he does not claim that all people would be better off without them. For those not guided by reason, pity can encourage concern for others, humility can restrain one from becoming ungovernably proud, and repentance can help one to avoid repeating mistakes. Spinoza thus allows for moral next-bests on the way to true liberation.

Nevertheless, it is very clear that the goal is to approximate as far as possible the model of human nature, and this exemplar would not yield to these passions. It seems that Spinoza intends to give us a sketch of this model of human nature when he turns at the end of *Ethics* part 4 to discuss the free person (*homo liber*), who "is led by reason" and who "complies with no one's wishes but his own, and does only those things he knows to be most important in life, and therefore desires very greatly" (4p66s). Among the things that we learn about the life of the free person are that she or he: thinks of nothing less than of death; has no knowledge of good or evil; avoids dangers; forms the strongest friendships; always acts honestly; and seeks to live in a strong state, rather than in solitude. Spinoza also tells us that such a person "hates no one, is angry with no one, envies no one, is indignant with no one, scorns no one, and is not at all proud" (4p73s).

While the picture of how the free person acts is fairly clear, if thin on details, interpretative questions persist concerning the function of the free man. For instance, scholars have debated whether the free person is in fact the model of human nature mentioned in the preface to *Ethics* part 4, and if this is even a coherent ideal. If the free person acts only from the dictates of reason, in what sense is this really a human at all since all human beings are necessarily susceptible to passions? Others have noted that even if the free person is a model of rationality, or a standard against which we can measure our virtue, it does not follow that we should always imitate the model.[22] After all, even if an ideally intelligent human being would not have to study for a logic exam, it does not mean that a philosophy student should not. This leaves us to ask to what extent we should look to the free person for guidance.[23] But while certain questions concerning the role of the free person in Spinoza's ethical system stand in need of interpretation, there can be no doubt that the free person passages give us a glimpse of what a flourishing life would be like for Spinoza: it is intellectual, cheerful, life affirming, upright, civic oriented, and characterized by the deepest forms of friendship.

Cognitive therapy

The fifth and final part of the *Ethics*, in which Spinoza considers "the means, or way, leading to freedom," divides fairly neatly into two sections. The first concerns the cognitive therapy, or the account of how reason gains control over the passions; the second concerns the greatest expression of human freedom: the intellectual love of God.

Spinoza opens his discussion of cognitive therapy by focusing on some of the ways in which we can gain control over the passions by clarifying our understanding of things. He claims that "[a]n affect which is a passion ceases to be a passion as soon as we form a clear and distinct idea of it" (5p3). Some commentators have thought that it is paradoxical to suggest that we can somehow convert a passion into an action, since passions arise through external causes, while adequate ideas do not. As Bennett memorably expresses the problem: one cannot form an adequate idea of a passion any more than one "can become royal by altering who [one's] parents were."[24] To see that there is nothing paradoxical about forming adequate ideas of passions, we must distinguish ideas of ideas, or second-order ideas, from the first-order ideas of which they are about. While passions, like anger or hate, are first-order ideas of a change in one's body's power of acting and of the putative cause, the clear and distinct ideas of passions that Spinoza refers to in 5p3 are second-order ideas: they are ideas *of* the first-order ideas. And there is nothing paradoxical about forming an adequate second-order idea of an inadequate first-order idea.

Still, this account does not explain how it is that the passion itself (the first-order idea) would be replaced by the adequate idea of it. Imagine, for instance, that one feels envious of a colleague who receives an award. One might come to understand this affective episode through the nature of envy itself[25] – the propensity for which is common to all humans – and thereby form a clear and distinct idea of it (5p4). But even then it would seem that the emotion itself could persist. Spinoza's point is probably that to the extent that the adequate idea engages the mind, the envy itself will occupy one's thinking less. This shows, once again, that for Spinoza the path to wisdom and freedom depends very much on the power or intensity of the ideas of which our mind is comprised. Viewed in this light, Spinoza's account resembles certain forms of mindfulness practice today that encourage one to observe one's affective states, rather than merely react on their basis.

The discussion of destroying love or hate by coming to "separate" the passions from "the thought of an external cause" (5p2) looks like another form of mindfulness. While Spinoza does not flesh out the psychological picture of what it means to separate the external cause from the affect, presumably it would consist in learning to distinguish the joy or sadness from the object which one takes to be the cause. So, if one's toe is stepped on while standing in a crowded train, one feels the pain *and* blames the putative cause of this pain. The feeling of anger or indignation is a secondary form of suffering. But if one could learn to separate the effect (in this case, the pain) from the putative cause (the aggressor), one could perhaps diminish the suffering that arises from focusing on the putative cause and thereby gain greater control over the affects.

This separation method helps to correct for our tendency to attribute too much to the presumed proximate external cause of the emotion, treating it as a free cause, which results in a more intense affective response (5p5). Coming to appreciate that all things are necessitated also helps to erode the power of the passions (5p6), as it enables us to be less affected by *particular* external causes (5p6d, 3p48), as we learn instead to trace these passions to an "infinite connection of causes" (5p6d). This, too, is confirmed experientially. If one learns that the train jostled the person who stepped on one's toe, one's affective reaction to this person will be lessened. And even if it is intentional, if one understands that the desire to harm others arises only from confused ideas that are themselves necessitated, one is likely to respond more forgivingly. As Spinoza notes earlier in the *Ethics*, the view that everything and everyone acts in accordance with natural necessity teaches us to "hate no one, to disesteem no one, to mock no one, to be angry at no one, to envy no one" (2p49s).

Even some of Spinoza's more sympathetic readers found the implication that this would render all vicious actions blameless to be disconcerting. His astute correspondent Tschirnhaus worried that, if Spinoza is right, "all wickedness would be excusable" (Ep. 57). Spinoza's reply is: "[W]hat of it? For evil men are no less to be feared, nor are they any less harmful, when they are necessarily evil" (Ep. 58). He elaborates on this point in a 1676 letter to Oldenburg, who also worries that Spinoza's view makes all actions excusable:

> Indeed, men can be excusable, and nevertheless lack blessedness and suffer in many ways. [...] Someone who is crazy because of a dog's bite is indeed to be excused; nevertheless, he is rightly suffocated. And finally, one who cannot govern his desires and restrain them by fear of the laws, although he too is to be excused because of his weakness, nevertheless, cannot enjoy peace of mind, and the knowledge and love of God. He necessarily perishes. (Ep. 78)

The blamelessness of vice does not imply that there is no reason to avoid wicked actions or that society need not protect itself against criminality. Learning to overcome misguided attributions of blame rids one of destructive, painful emotions like anger, hatred, resentment, and so forth, without undermining one's motivation for cultivating virtue in oneself or promoting it in others.

Nevertheless, developing the habits of thought that enable one to limit the power of the passions – through forming clear and distinct ideas of them, detaching the emotion from the putative cause, and perceiving things as necessary and blameless – is something that can only be achieved with great effort. Once again, Spinoza's approach resembles contemporary mindfulness techniques like those deployed in forms of cognitive-behavioral therapy. He calls for a form of mental reconditioning whereby one meditates on certain key truths, imprinting them on one's memory so that they are ready to hand:

> The best thing, then, that we can do, so long as we do not have perfect knowledge of our affects, is to conceive a correct principle of living, *or* sure maxims of life, to commit them to memory, and to apply them constantly to the particular cases frequently encountered in life. In this way our imagination will be extensively affected by them, and we shall always have them ready. For example, we have laid it down as a maxim of life (see 4p46 and p46s) that hate is to be conquered by love, or nobility, not by repaying it with hate in return. But in order that we may always have this rule ready when it is needed, we ought to think about and meditate frequently on the common wrongs of men, and how they may be warded off best by nobility. For if we join the image of a wrong to the imagination of this maxim, it will always be ready for us (by 2p18) when a wrong is done to us. If we have ready also the principle of our own true advantage, and also of the good which follows from mutual friendship and common society, and keep in mind, moreover, that the highest satisfaction of mind stems from the right principle of living (by 4p52), and that men, like other things, act from the necessity of nature, then the wrong, or the hate usually arising from it, will occupy a very small part of the imagination, and will easily be overcome. (5p10s)

This meditative reconditioning is key to enacting the remedies that Spinoza describes. Even though it has drawn its fair share of criticism,[26] his cognitive therapy is, in the end, quite intelligible and in line with recent developments in psychology. By impressing on the imagination one's understanding of the nature of hatred, its origin, and its futility and destructive power, one will be prepared when confronted with hostile people not simply to respond in kind but to act more mindfully, understandingly, and rationally. But while this account of how we gain rational control over our passions is clearly a key part of the path to liberation, there is yet a higher expression of human freedom, one that comes only through the third kind of knowledge and the intellectual love of God.

6.5 Individual eternity and the highest good

The critical fire drawn by the first half of the final part of the *Ethics* pales in comparison to that received by the latter half, the capstone of Spinoza's moral philosophy.[27] Given its abstract nature and lofty ambitions, this is perhaps unsurprising. However, a careful and charitable interpretation of the latter half reveals that it is quite consistent with the rest of the book.[28]

Here our first task is to figure out what Spinoza means by the eternity of the mind. As we have seen, there are two kinds of ideas: adequate and inadequate. By "imagination," Spinoza refers to the inadequate first kind of cognition, which includes sensory perception, hearsay, and symbolic association (2p40s2). "The intellect," by contrast, encompasses ideas that arise from second and third kinds of knowledge – ideas that one has insofar as one grasps things adequately (2p40s2, 5p10d). The imagination comprises all, and only, inadequate ideas, while the intellect comprises all, and only, adequate ideas. Moreover, imagination is purely passive, intellect active. Also, their objects are distinct. The object of the imagination is the actually existing human body (2p13) – that is, the body insofar as it has a finite, determinate existence or duration (1p21d). Consequently, one imagines things only as long as the body endures since the imagination is the part of the mind that is destroyed with the destruction of the actually existing body (5p21). But Spinoza also famously and puzzlingly states that "it is time now to pass to those things which pertain to the mind's duration without relation to the body" (5p20s). Given what he has earlier taught us about the relation between mind and body, the standard worry has been that here Spinoza violates his own principles: how could the mind be severed from the body in this way?

In the discussion that ensues, Spinoza reveals that there is an "eternal part of the mind," which is nothing but the intellect (5p40c, 5p40s). If the object of the imagination is the actually existing body, what is the object of the intellect? Here we should recall the distinction between two types of essences: actual and formal.[29] The former is an individual's essence as it is constituted in the constantly varying circumstances of the durational existence. The latter has proven to be something of an interpretative puzzle, but the following proposition and its corollary contain the critical pieces of information:

> The ideas of singular things, *or of modes*, that do not exist must be comprehended in God's infinite idea in the same way as the formal essences of the singular things, *or* modes, are contained in God's attributes. (2p8)

> From this it follows that so long as singular things do not exist, *except insofar as they are comprehended in God's attributes*, their objective being, or ideas, do not exist except insofar as God's infinite idea exists. And when singular things are said to exist, *not only insofar as they are comprehended in God's attributes, but insofar also as they are said*

to have duration, their ideas also involve the existence through which they are said to have duration. (2p8c, emphases added)

While 2p8 underscores the distinction between the formal essence and actual existence of a singular thing, 2p8c indicates that a thing's formal essence – and the corresponding divine idea thereof – has its own form of existence. Unlike the *actual* existence of a singular thing, the existence corresponding to a singular thing's formal essence is eternal. And in 2p45s, Spinoza makes it clear that the eternal existence of singular things "insofar as they are in God" – that is, the (formal) essences of things themselves – is the privileged form of existence.[30] This form of existence is utterly distinct from existence in time, and it forms the basis of the individuality of finite things. This is a debated and difficult issue, but we believe that it can be said that the formal essence is, as it were, the unchanging blueprint each individual strives to realize with its intrinsic power – and thereby the ontological feature that individuates the power.[31]

This dual-existence reading sheds light on the discussion of the eternity of the mind in the final part of the *Ethics*. The demonstration of the proposition that "[t]he human mind cannot be absolutely destroyed with the body, but something of it remains which is eternal" (5p23) invokes the two forms of existence:

> In God there is necessarily a concept, *or* idea, which expresses the essence of the human body (by p22), an idea, therefore, which is necessarily something that pertains to the essence of the human mind (by 2p13). But we do not attribute to the human mind any duration that can be defined by time, except insofar as it expresses the actual existence of the body, which is explained by duration, and can be defined by time, that is (by 2p8c), we do not attribute duration to it except while the body endures. However, since what is conceived, with a certain eternal necessity, through God's essence itself (by p22) is *nevertheless something*, this *something that pertains to the essence of the mind will necessarily be eternal*[.] (5p23d, emphasis added)

Even when the determinate existence of the body comes to an end, one still exists in some sense because one's formal essence is inscribed in God's attributes. And the corresponding idea of this formal essence in God's intellect is one's eternal mind.

This leaves us with the question of how to understand the claim that, during our actual existence, our mind can be more or less eternal. The answer lies in the idea that we can be, and inevitably are, more or less active, with activity linked to eternally true ideas, passivity to inadequate and confused ideas. Their relationship in our mind is of utmost importance:

> [T]hat mind is most acted on, of which inadequate ideas constitute the greatest part, so that it is distinguished more by what it undergoes than by what it does. On the other hand, that mind acts most, of which adequate ideas constitute the greatest part, so that though it may have as many inadequate ideas as the other, it is still distinguished more by those which are attributed to human virtue than by those which betray man's lack of power. (5p20s)

Slightly later, Spinoza argues that "the more the mind understands things by the second and third kind of knowledge, the greater part of it remains [after the destruction of the actually existing body]" (5p38d). The striving for understanding is ultimately a striving for the intellect to predominate over the imagination, or for our adequate ideas to overpower or restrain the passions. It is not enough to *have* adequate ideas; once again, they must be powerful. This explains why large stretches of the two final parts of the *Ethics* are devoted to analyzing the determinants of the intensity of ideas (4p5–p16, 5p5–p13). The view of cognitive achievement as the intensification of adequate ideas is reflected in several passages in the final part of the *Ethics*, including the following:

> [F]or although I have shown generally in part 1 that all things (and consequently the human mind also) depend on God both for their essence and their existence, nevertheless, that demonstration, though legitimate and put beyond all chance of doubt, still does not affect our mind as much as when this is inferred from the very essence of any singular thing which we say depends on God. (5p36s)

Spinoza's point here is that the third kind of knowledge is superior to the second in part because it is more powerful – it "affects the mind" more. To know things in this way is to have a *powerful* intellect, so that adequate ideas of eternal truths affect or engage the mind more than the passions and the imagination. To succeed in this is our central cognitive task, something we are to achieve in this life.

However, even if one considered Spinoza's framework compelling – as foreign as it is bound to appear to our predominantly secular age – there remains a profound and perhaps deeply troubling question: to what extent is the immortal or eternal existence that Spinoza describes immortality *for us*? Since so much of what we experience in this lifetime – all our sense perceptions, memories, feelings, etc. – is tied to the actual body, which perishes when we die and is utterly disconnected from our eternal essence (5p21), it cannot be that we experience some form of *personal* immortality.[32] In other words, after we die, there remains no *me* that could enjoy anything even vaguely resembling the delights depicted by, for instance, the traditional Christian view.

Still, this does not diminish the importance of our cognitive efforts. Spinoza makes a distinction between two very different types of epistemic positions:

> We conceive things as actual in two ways: either insofar as we conceive them to exist in relation to a certain time and place, or insofar as we conceive them to be contained in God and to follow from the necessity of the divine nature. But the things we conceive in this second way as true, *or* real, we conceive under a species of eternity, and to that extent they involve the eternal and infinite essence of God (as we have shown in 2p45 and p45s). (5p29s)

As we come to know things more adequately, we more fully realize the power of our essence, and we grasp things more as God does, without relation to time. We thereby "participate" more in eternity just in the sense that we more fully realize our essence, apprehending things "under a species of eternity" (*sub specie aeternitatis*) – ultimately, by the cognitively superior third kind of knowledge.

On this view becoming more eternal is not without its very concrete joys – it is just that they concern *this life*, not our eternal existence. Whatever salvation or enhanced eternity one achieves in this lifetime expires along with one's determinate existence. In line with this, Spinoza famously states that "[b]lessedness is not the reward of virtue, but virtue itself" (5p42). This makes sense because as we have seen, virtuous striving is rational striving, which increases our perfection. Thus: "[H]e who knows things by this kind of knowledge passes to the greatest human perfection, and consequently (by defaff2), is affected with the greatest joy, accompanied (by 2p43) by the idea of himself and his virtue. Therefore (by defaff25), the greatest satisfaction there can be arises from this kind of knowledge" (5p27d).

Here, one notable circle closes. The young Spinoza begins the *Treatise on the Emendation of the Intellect* with a passionate manifesto to find out the greatest good available to human beings; the final pages of the *Ethics* can be seen as an elated celebration having found the source of lasting joy. Given that it arises from understanding God or Nature, which is thus the ultimate cause of this bliss,[33] Spinoza could ask, how could we *not* love it? The famed intellectual love of God (*amor Dei intellectualis*) Spinoza introduces in 5p32–p33 is thus only the natural emotional endpoint of his view of the highest human good.[34] From this we see that Spinoza's joy-centered moral philosophy does not reduce to boorish hedonism since it is the cultivation of the mind – particularly, coming to know and love God – that supplies the most lasting and powerful joy.

Further reading

Garrett, Don. 2018. *Nature and Necessity in Spinoza's Philosophy*. Oxford: Oxford University Press, chs 9, 16–18.

Kisner, Matthew J. 2011. *Spinoza on Human Freedom*. Cambridge: Cambridge University Press.

Kisner, Matthew J. and Youpa, Andrew (eds). 2014. *Essays on Spinoza's Ethical Theory*. Oxford: Oxford University Press.

LeBuffe, Michael. 2010. *From Bondage to Freedom: Spinoza on Human Excellence*. Oxford: Oxford University Press.

Nadler, Steven. 2001. *Spinoza's Heresy: Immortality and the Jewish Mind*. Oxford: Clarendon Press.

Youpa, Andrew. 2020. *The Ethics of Joy: Spinoza on the Empowered Life*. Oxford: Oxford University Press.

7

Political Philosophy

One puzzle that readers of Spinoza's full corpus must confront is why the author of the *Ethics*, a work that advocates rational control over the passions and encourages us to conceive of things from the eternal perspective, should devote much of the last decade of his life to writing about politics, which are dominated by passions and which are explicitly concerned with the here and now. If the *Ethics* invites us to take up things as timeless and necessary, politics seems to plunge us back into the realm of history, corruptibility, and fortune. In this chapter, we will try to show how the political works can be seen as an extension of, rather than a departure from, the *Ethics*.[1]

7.1 Political context

We have already looked at the theological and political context behind the composition of the TTP.[2] We noted that the work, published in 1670, was written as a response to the threat to philo-sophical freedom posed by the politically empowered Calvinist clergy, as evidenced through the imprisonment and subsequent death of Spinoza's friend Adriaan Koerbagh. It was also in some sense an intervention on a decades-long struggle in the Netherlands between liberals and Calvinist hardliners over the place of religion in politics. The first 15 chapters of the work can be seen as an elaborate argument for the separation of faith from philosophy. The last five chapters of the work (16–20) – the contents of which will be examined below – are more directly concerned with politics, culminating in an argument for the indispensability of the freedom to philosophize. In the end, though, the TTP did not impact Dutch political discourse, much less influence public policy. Responses to the TTP tended to be highly critical, focusing on the perceived antireligiosity of the work.

The situation for freethinkers in the Netherlands did not get any better in the immediate aftermath to the publication of the TTP. Liberal republicans were dealt a major blow in 1672. In this so-called "disaster year" (*rampjaar*), French troops, under the command of Louis XIV, invaded the United Provinces, capturing a number of Dutch cities.[3] The Grand Pensionary, Johan de Witt, shouldered much of the blame for this military embarrassment. After the invasion, the stadtholdership was reinstituted in the person of William III, and De Witt was forced to resign. Shortly thereafter, he and his brother, Cornelis, were brutally murdered by a zealous mob. This incident so outraged Spinoza that, according to one famous account, Spinoza had to be restrained by his landlord from taking a sign reading *ultimi barbarorum* or "ultimate of barbarians" to the site of the massacre.[4] Spinoza's *Tractatus Politicus* (TP) was composed in the wake of these events.

It is natural to wonder why Spinoza wrote a second political treatise. Did the events of 1672 prompt Spinoza to change his views about political life? Some have thought so, proposing for instance that he grew disenchanted with democracy, after seeing what the mob did to the De Witt brothers.[5] However, careful inspection of the later political treatise reveals that it is every bit as democratic in its outlook as the TTP. In fact, with the possible exception of his views concerning the social contract, there is little evidence that Spinoza came to reject any of the central claims of his earlier treatise.

The primary ways in which the two political treatises differ is in terms of their rhetorical style and aims. The rhetorical differences can be explained by their distinct target audiences. The TTP was published anonymously and written for an audience of liberal Christian theologians. By contrast, the TP, which remained unfinished at the time of Spinoza's death in 1677, was written for philosophers. The aims of the works are also distinct. While the TTP seeks to protect the citizenry from ideological corruption by curbing the power of the clergy and limiting the scope of sovereign intervention, the TP seeks to identify institutions that promote civic integration and collective rationality. The TTP has a kind of methodological pride of place, since no good institutions can be erected as long as superstition and persecution persist, while the TP completes the ambitions of the *Ethics*, revealing the extent to which individual freedom depends on civic institutions.

Ultimately, we should not be surprised to find Spinoza's philosophy taking a civic turn near the end of his life. From his earliest writings, he claims that he is concerned not just to perfect his own nature but also "to form a society of the kind that is desirable, so that as many as possible may attain [a flourishing life] as easily and surely as possible" (TIE, §14). The political treatises may be seen as Spinoza's attempt to articulate some of the conditions for the possibility of such a society.

Before we turn to the contents of his political treatises, it will be helpful to say a bit about the political thinkers whose work most directly influenced Spinoza. Among the most important local influences were the De la Court brothers. Pieter and Johan de la Court were ardent republicans who maintained good relations with Johan de Witt.[6] They proposed the adoption of institutional measures, such as the use of blind balloting, the removal of hereditary posts, and the rotation of offices that would keep the interests of governors tied to the interests of the governed. Spinoza evidently studied these works carefully, and his institutional recommendations in the TP reflect his debt to the De la Courts.[7]

The De la Courts also helped to introduce Machiavelli's political thought to the Dutch Republic, and in this way too they likely influenced Spinoza. The *Political Treatise* is a deeply Machiavellian work, especially in terms of its method. At the outset of the work, Spinoza echoes Machiavelli's critique of utopian theorizing, claiming that statespersons are better suited to give advice than philosophers since the former, unlike the latter, begin with a realistic conception of human psychology (TP 1/1).[8] Like Machiavelli, Spinoza believed that one must properly identify the roots of civil problems before one can offer useful prescriptions for overcoming them. Machiavellian realism underlies much of the constitutional theorizing of the TP.

Machiavelli's influence on Spinoza's political philosophy is rivalled only by Hobbes's. Spinoza read Hobbes's *De Cive* carefully, and he might also have read *Leviathan*, which appeared in Latin in 1668, as Spinoza was completing the TTP. We will consider Spinoza's work in relationship to Hobbes throughout. Here we will simply note that, as was the case for Machiavelli, there was a Dutch conduit for Hobbesian thought, namely the anticlerical physician Lambert van Velthuysen. Velthuysen's *Dissertatio* is an unabashed defense of Hobbes's thought. Spinoza read and admired Velthuysen as a person "possessed only by a zeal for the truth" (Ep. 69), and was thus disconcerted when Velthuysen denounced the TTP as the work of an atheist (Epp. 42–3).

7.2 Right, obligation, and power

Having briefly situated the context of Spinoza's political writings, we may now turn to his specific claims. At the heart of both of his political treatises is a bracing critique of traditional natural jurisprudence. While medieval and early modern theorists of natural right and law disagreed amongst themselves about the exact nature of the source and content of natural right and law, they shared a fundamental commitment to the view that there is a natural order of rights and obligations distinct from the actual order of events. We may call this the double order of Nature view. The double order of Nature made it possible for one to act contrary to the natural law or perform actions without right.

We have seen that Spinoza rejects the double order view of Nature,[9] just as he rejects the view of a divine legislator with a will distinct from his intellect. On his view, everything that exists is causally determined by God's nature and the laws inscribed therein. These laws of nature are necessary and unchanging, as there is no order outside of Nature that could alter or oppose them. To conceive of God as legislator is to conceive of a being with a will distinct from its intellect, a creative power distinct from its nature, which is to ascribe to God a power outside of his power, or a nature outside of Nature. This is patently at odds with monism. Rather that dispensing with juridical language, though, he replaces normative conceptions of right and law with naturalistic proxies. We see this in his treatment both of natural right and natural law.

One of the most notorious aspects of Spinoza's political thought is his account of natural right. He introduces this concept in TTP 16, where he boldly writes:

> By the right and established practice of nature I mean nothing but the rules of the nature of each individual, according to which we conceive each thing to be naturally determined to existing and having effects in a certain way. For example, fish are determined by nature to swimming, and the large ones to eating the smaller. So it is by the supreme right of nature that fish are masters of the water, and that the large ones eat the smaller. For it's certain that nature, considered absolutely, has the supreme right to do everything it can,

i.e., that the right of nature extends as far as its power does. For the power of nature is the power of God itself, and he has the supreme right over all things. But the universal power of the whole of nature is nothing but the power of all individuals together. From this it follows that each individual has a supreme right to do everything it can, or that right of each thing extends as far as its determinate power does. (TTP 16.2–3; G III, 189)

The main claim here, that one's right extends as far and only as far as one's power extends, is sometimes called the coextensivity thesis. Roughly the same argument – supplemented by a better account of the relationship between God and particular things – appears in the TP (2/2–2/4). Here Spinoza argues that because anything that an individual does, it does from God's power, and because everything done from God's power is done by right, everything that an individual does, it does by right.

In claiming that the right of nature is coextensive with the power of nature and that this applies *mutatis mutandis* to the individuals in nature, Spinoza is straightforwardly rejecting the view that there is an independent juridical order – a nature outside of nature – on the basis of which we may declare an action just or unjust, legitimate or illegitimate. To say that something is done by right in Spinoza's sense is not to make a positive normative claim; rather, it is just to say that there is nothing in virtue of which that action can be judged impermissible. So, even if Cortés conquered the Aztecs by right, it does not follow that it is sanctioned or permissible; rather, the point is that this action does not violate any natural juridical order, since there is no such order. Spinoza adopts the language of right only to drain it of its normative significance.

Spinoza does something similar with the concept of natural law. Rather than conceiving of laws as violable edicts of a superior power, Spinoza defines law in the most general sense as that by which things "act in one and the same fixed and determinate way" (TTP 4.1; G III, 57). God does not issue laws through a decree; rather, the laws of nature are just the operations of Nature itself. Anything one does, one does in accordance with these very laws, which are "eternal and can't be violated" (TP 2/18), and which "[prohibit] nothing except what no one can do" (TP 2/18).[10]

The idea of a natural law as a violable command of God can thus only be a product of misapprehension and confusion. This point is vividly illustrated in Spinoza's interpretation of the parable of Adam. Spinoza thinks that it is absurd to suppose that Adam actually acted contrary to God's command not to eat the forbidden fruit because nothing can act contrary to God's laws. Rather, on Spinoza's idiosyncratic rendering, what was "revealed" to Adam was a necessary law – namely, "eating fruit from this tree will result in such-and-such consequences" – that Adam, in his ignorance, took to be a command (TTP 4.26–7; G III, 63). Spinoza expressed these same ideas in a letter he wrote in 1665, roughly a half-decade before the publication of the TTP:

> For because [will] does not differ from [God's] intellect, it is as impossible for something to happen contrary to his will as it would be for something to happen contrary to his intellect. I.e., what would happen contrary to his will must be of such a nature that it conflicts with his intellect, like a square circle. [...] [I]n this way the prophets wrote a whole parable. First, because god had revealed the means to salvation and destruction, and was the cause of them, they represented him as a king and lawgiver. The means, which are nothing but causes, they called laws and wrote in the manner of laws. Salvation and destruction, which are nothing but effects which follow from the means, they represented as reward and punishment. They have ordered all their words more according to this parable than according to the truth. Throughout they have represented god as a man, now angry, now merciful, now longing for the future, now seized by jealousy and suspicion, indeed even deceived by the devil. [...] The prohibition to Adam, then, consisted only in this: god revealed to Adam that eating of that tree caused death, just as he also reveals to us through the natural intellect that poison is deadly to us. (Ep. 19; G IV, 90–3)

On this striking account, God's "decrees" are nothing but the necessary, inviolable laws of Nature. Once again, then, Spinoza undercuts traditional conceptions of natural law by rejecting the double order of nature.

The closest predecessor to Spinoza with respect to natural jurisprudence was Hobbes. Hobbes's account of natural right has been the subject of much interpretative dispute. In *De Cive*, he defines right as "that liberty which each man hath to make use of his natural faculties according to right reason" (*De Cive* I.7; EW II, 9). In other words, natural right is the liberty to do anything consistent with the natural law. This includes the right to do anything that one judges to be necessary for one's preservation (*De Cive* I.8–9; EW II, 9). Hobbes adds a proviso here, namely that one violates the law of nature, or acts without right, when one acts in a way that one does not sincerely believe contributes to one's preservation (*De Cive* I.10; EW II, 10). And later Hobbes suggests that because "drunkenness or cruelty" cannot sincerely be thought to contribute to self-preservation, drunken and cruel actions are not performed by right, even in the state of nature (*De Cive* III.27; EW II, 45).

In *Leviathan*, however, Hobbes seems to advance an account of natural right that is not bound by such normative constraints. He defines *right of nature* as "the liberty each man hath, to use his own power, as he will himself, for the preservation of his own nature; that is to say, of his own life; and consequently, of doing any thing, which in his own judgement, and reason, he shall conceive to be the aptest means thereunto" (*Leviathan* I.14; EW III, 116). Still, Hobbes is committed to the view that natural right is distinct from power since the former can be transferred, while the latter cannot; and the transference of right gives rise to obligations. The creation of a moral juridical order that is distinct from the actual order of events is essential to Hobbes's account of sovereign authority and civil obligation.

Spinoza distances himself from Hobbes on this crucial point. When asked in a letter from his friend Jarig Jellesz what sets his views apart from Hobbes's, Spinoza wrote: "As far as politics is concerned, the difference you ask about, between Hobbes and me, is this: I always preserve natural right unimpaired, and I maintain that in each state the supreme magistrate has no more right over its subjects than it has greater power over them" (Ep. 50).

While the transferability or alienability of one's natural right to judge how to defend oneself serves as the foundation of Hobbes's political theory, Spinoza sees this as a violation of naturalism.

Spinoza's skepticism about normative rights leads him also to reject the account of obligation found in Hobbes. Whereas Hobbes suggests that we incur binding obligations through the trans-ference of right, Spinoza baldly asserts that "a contract can have no force except by reason of its utility. If the utility is taken away, the contract is taken away with it, and remains null and void" (TTP 16.20; G III, 192).[11] To demand that people act contrary to perceived utility is to demand the impossible since "it's a universal law of human nature that no one neglects to pursue what he judges to be good, unless he hopes for a greater good, or fears a greater harm [...][;] [b]etween two goods, each person chooses the one he judges to be greater, between two evils, the one which seems to him lesser" (TTP 16.15; G III, 191–2). Interestingly enough, in a passage from *De Cive* in which he explains why we cannot covenant not to resist the penalty of death, Hobbes seems to embrace this very argument:

> [B]y the contract of not resisting, we are obliged, of two evils to make choice of that which seems the greater. For certain death is a greater evil than fighting. But of two evils it is impossible not to choose least. By such a compact, therefore, we should be tied to impossibilities; which is contrary to the very nature of compacts. (*De Cive* II.18; EW II, 26)

But Hobbes does not fully pursue the implications of this claim. To do so would be to concede that one cannot alienate one's right to judge what conduces to one's welfare since this too is psychologically impossible. This would undermine the very foundation on which Hobbes's account of obligation is built. At least in this respect, Spinoza may be said to be a more thoroughgoing naturalist than Hobbes.

Naturalizing authority

But even if Spinoza rejects the double order of Nature, he does not deny the reality of a distinct political domain, characterized by sovereign authority or right and obligatory civil laws. How can we reconcile his claim that one always preserves one's natural right with the existence of a sovereign authority to which all members of a state are subject? Otherwise put, what does it mean to stand under the right of another, if right is coextensive with power and power is nontransferable?

To answer this, it is helpful to distinguish between two concepts that are translated into English as "power": *potentia* and *potestas*.[12] *Potentia* refers to one's incommunicable causal power, while *potestas* refers to something more like authority. Even if one cannot transfer one's *potentia* to another, one can stand under the *potestas* of another. Spinoza describes how in both of his political treatises. Here is his account from the TP:

> One person has another in his power [a] if he has him tied up, or [b] if he has taken away his arms and means of defending himself or escaping, or [c] if he has instilled fear in him, or [d] if he has so bound him to himself by a benefit that the other person would rather conduct himself according to his benefactor's wishes than according to his own, and wants to live according to his benefactor's opinion, not according to his own. (TP 2/10)[13]

The final example, of one who would "rather conduct himself according to his benefactor's wishes than according to his own" because of some perceived benefit, is especially important since it suggests that one can act from the power or right of another even when one is directly pursuing one's own perceived utility. Acting from the right of another is perfectly consistent with doing what one wishes, free from coercion. Indeed, Spinoza seems to think that the best states are characterized by such willing, hopeful compliance. Authority, on Spinoza's view, is perfectly compatible with acting from one's own judgment and interest. This point is perhaps best captured by the following passage from the TTP:

> [T]o understand rightly how far the right and power of the state extend, we must note that its power is not limited to what it can compel men to do from fear, but extends to absolutely everything it can bring men to do in compliance with its commands. [...] For whatever reason a man resolves to carry out the commands of the supreme power, whether because he fears punishment, or because he hopes for something from it, or because he loves his country, or because he has been impelled by any other affect whatever, he still forms his resolution according to his own judgment, notwithstanding that he acts in accordance with the command of the supreme power. *So we must not infer simply from the fact that a man does something by his own judgment, that he does it by his own right, and not by the right of the state. For since he always acts by his own judgment and decision – both when he is bound by love and when he is compelled by fear to avoid some evil – if there is to be a state and a right over subjects, political authority must extend to everything which can bring men to decide to yield to it.* So whatever a subject does which answers to the commands of the supreme power – whether he's been bound by love, or compelled by fear, or (as indeed is more frequent) by hope and fear together, whether he acts from reverence (a passion composed of fear and wonder) or is led by any reason whatever – he acts by the right of the state, not his own right. (TTP 17.5–7; G III, 201–2, emphasis added)

While Hobbes claims that sovereignty requires that one transfer away the right to judge how best to preserve oneself, in this passage Spinoza asserts that if political authority required the alienation of a subject's power to judge, the commonwealth could not exist. He instead understands authority and subjection in terms of a dependency relationship in virtue of which the subject's actions are either directly compelled by the authority or are counterfactually dependent such that if the subject did not believe that she were satisfying some demand, request, or desire of the other, then she would not have acted as she did. This allows Spinoza to maintain that one can retain one's right (as *potentia*), while subjecting oneself to the authority (*potestas*) of another.

This way of conceiving the formation of authority shows why an apparent difference between the two political treatises matters far less than some readers have supposed. In the TTP, Spinoza gives a contract-based account of the generation of the commonwealth, claiming that in order to escape a condition of misery, people had to "make a very firm resolution and contract to direct everything only according to the dictate of reason" (TTP 16.14; G III, 191). And he proceeds to illustrate this through his account of the Hebrew state, in which "everyone surrendered his right equally, as in a democracy, and they cried out in one voice 'whatever God says' (without any explicit mediator) 'we will do'" (TTP 17.33; G III, 206). However, in the *Political Treatise*, he dispenses with the apparatus of the contract, claiming instead to "deduce" the formation of the state from human nature as it actually is (TP 1/4). In our view, this distinction is not especially significant since, as Spinoza himself notes, sovereign authority does not depend on having any particular genesis: "For us to recognize [sovereigns'] right, it's not necessary now to know what their origin is or how they often arise" (TTP 16.37; G III, 195). Rather, what matters is that a certain dependency relationship obtains between the sovereign body and the subjects.

The significance of Spinoza's critique of natural jurisprudence

Spinoza's critique of natural jurisprudence reveals something very important about his normative political project. Proponents of natural jurisprudence contend that there are constraints on what one may do in the pursuit of interests. By casting off juridical constraints, Spinoza places the burden of political stability squarely on the sovereign. The ruling body cannot simply appeal to a normative conception of right to demand compliance; rather, it must work to ensure that subjects perceive obedience as in their interest. And when there is excessive vice or non-compliance, Spinoza claims that the blame must be "imputed to the common-wealth" (TP 5/3). So, whereas Hobbes argues that the sovereign is vested with (nearly) absolute legislative authority, Spinoza claims that "[b]ecause the commonwealth's right is defined by the common power of a multitude, it's certain that its power and right are diminished to the extent that it provides many people with reasons to conspire against it" (TP 3/9). The state must win the loyalty of the people in order to maintain its right or power.

7.3 The aim of politics

While Spinoza does not embrace the framework of natural right and natural law, this does not mean that he lacks a normative political theory. In chapter 5 of the TP, he explicitly distinguishes between acting from right and doing something well:

> In [TP] 2/11, we showed that a man is most his own master when he is led most by reason, and so (by 3/7) that a commonwealth is most powerful, and most its own master, when it's founded on and directed by reason. [...] For when we say that someone has done something by right, we're not saying he's done it in the best way. It's one thing to cultivate a field by right and another to cultivate it in the best way. It's also, I say, one thing to defend oneself, preserve oneself, make a judgment, etc., by right, and another to defend oneself, preserve oneself, and make a judgment in the best way. So, it's one thing to command and have responsibility for public affairs by right, and another to command and govern public affairs in the best way. (TP 5/1)

He then precedes to claim that the "end" or "aim" of the state – the norm for measuring civic health, as it were – is "peace and security of life" (TP 5/2). In the TTP, he construes the aim of the state somewhat differently, claiming that "the end of the republic is really freedom" (TTP 20.12; G III, 241). Since "freedom" looks like a loftier goal than simply "peace and security," one might wonder whether Spinoza's views concerning the aim of the state underwent a substantial revision between his two political treatises. We think that in fact these three stated aims of the state – peace, security, and freedom – describe a single civic condition. By examining Spinoza's understanding of what peace, security, and political freedom consist in, we will be able to see not only that these norms are consistent, but also how his account of the civic good coheres with his views about goodness more generally.[14]

Let us begin with the concept of peace. If one understands peace as Hobbes did, as the mere absence of war (*De Cive* I.12; EW II, 11), it looks like an extremely modest civic goal. However, Spinoza sharply rejects Hobbes's definition, claiming instead:

A commonwealth whose subjects, terrified by fear, don't take up arms should be said to be without war, but not at peace. Peace isn't the privation of war, but a virtue which arises from strength of mind. [...] When the peace of a commonwealth depends on its subjects' lack of spirit – so that they're led like sheep, and know only how to be slaves – it would be more properly called a wasteland than a commonwealth. When we say, then, that the best state is one where men pass their lives harmoniously, I mean that they pass a human life, one defined not merely by the circulation of the blood, and other things common to all animals, but mostly by reason, the true virtue and life of the mind. (TP 5/4–5)

Harmonious cooperation that arises out of reason or strength of mind is clearly not the same thing as mere stability or the absence of war. Spinoza illustrates the difference between peace and mere stability in his analysis of "the Turks" or the Ottoman Empire:

No state has stood so long without notable change as that of the Turks. [...] Still, if slavery, barbarism, and being without protection are to be called peace, nothing is more wretched for men than peace. No doubt there are more, and more bitter, quarrels between parents and children than between masters and slaves. Nevertheless, it doesn't make for the orderly management of a household to change paternal right into mastery, and treat children like slaves. To transfer all power to one man makes for bondage, not peace. As we've said, peace does not consist in the privation of war, but in a union *or* harmony of minds. (TP 6/4)

But if peace signifies a flourishing civil condition, marked by a "harmony of minds," one may wonder why Spinoza groups "peace" together with "security," which sounds like a much lower baseline.

Like peace, though, "security" (*securitas*) denotes far more than just protection from physical harm for Spinoza. It refers to a state of psychological wellbeing, a freedom from fear and anxiety. In the *Ethics*, Spinoza defines *securitas* as a stable form of hope – which is itself a species of joy – devoid of doubt and fear (defaff14; 3p18s2).[15] And the political writings drive home just how much better off a hopeful, secure people are than a fearful people.[16] Only in a state where fear has largely been replaced by firm hope, or security, is the civic ideal of peace genuinely possible.

Tellingly, in the passage from the TTP in which he announces that the purpose of the state is freedom, Spinoza links freedom with the diminution of fear and the establishment of security:

From the foundations of the republic explained above it follows most clearly that its ultimate end is not to dominate, restraining men by fear, and making them subject to another's control, but on the contrary to free each person from fear, so that he can live securely, as far as possible, i.e., so that he retains to the utmost his natural right to exist and operate without harm to himself or anyone else. The end of the republic, I say, is [...] to enable their minds and bodies to perform their functions safely, to enable them to use their reason freely[.] [...] [T]he end of the republic is really freedom. (TTP 20.11–12; G III, 240–1)

Political freedom, peace, and security refer to a condition of widespread hope or trust, in which subjects are able to cultivate their minds and act in rational concert. While this may sound rather quixotic for a philosopher who rails against utopian theorizing,[17] we should bear in mind here that Spinoza is describing an ideal condition. It might be no more possible for a real state to achieve *total* peace, freedom, and security than it is for a real human to become a free man.[18] Nevertheless, these are ideals that can be approximated and can be used as a measure of civic success.

This account of the aim of the state is very much in keeping with the account of goodness presented earlier.[19] There we saw that a thing is good for someone to the extent and only to the extent that it increases that being's power of acting or joy. Consequently, relative to the striving of its citizens, a state is good to the extent and only to the extent that it empowers its constituents. Peace, security, and freedom denote a condition of joy and empowerment. Having eliminated juridical side constraints through his critique of natural right, Spinoza is able to maintain that the state has a single directive: to liberate or empower its citizens as far as possible.

7.4 Toleration

Spinoza is often recognized for his contribution to the liberal tradition, due, in large part, to his defense of the freedom to philosophize in the concluding chapter of the TTP. Nevertheless, his arguments in defense of the freedoms of thought and speech are not often examined in much detail. As we shall see, his defense of the freedom to philosophize is multilayered, nuanced, and psychologically insightful. Unlike other prominent early modern defenders of toleration, like John Locke and Pierre Bayle, Spinoza's does not evince any doubt concerning religious and moral knowledge; consequently, he does not ground his defense of the freedom to philosophize in the epistemic parity of competing belief systems. Nor does he appeal to normative rights or moral titles in his defense of such freedoms since, as we have seen, he denies the existence of normative rights or titles. Again, the state has a single imperative, and that is to empower its citizens as far as possible. Freedom to philosophize must thus conduce to civic power. But why?

The anticlerical case for toleration

In the TTP, Spinoza provides both anticlerical and secular arguments for toleration. The anticlerical case is made in the first 19 chapters of the work, one main component of which is the Separation Thesis, which we explored earlier.[20] We will recall that the main point of the Separation Thesis is to show that religious faith does not aim at truth and therefore does not compete with philosophy as a source of metaphysical or ethical knowledge. While Spinoza claims to establish simply that faith and reason are not in conflict, in fact what he shows is that Scripture is at best a repository of moral tales and precepts that are useful for those who are incapable of understanding moral truths through philosophy. Moreover, because the moral truths of Scripture are immediately evident to all readers, there is no need for a priestly caste versed in the arts of hermeneutics to interpret the claims of the text for the masses. In this way, Spinoza undermines clerical and priestly authority.

While the Separation Thesis, defended in the first 15 chapters of the work, limits the intellectual authority of the clerics, chapters 16–19 complete the case against clerical power by denying it political authority. In these chapters, Spinoza argues, as Hobbes did before him, that sovereign authority is incompatible with a separate ecclesiastical authority. Essentially, he argues that a civil sovereign could not retain its power to legislate unless it also has authority over matters of faith, for if there were an independent religious authority, its authority could limit or even supersede the sovereign's (TTP 16.61–3, 19.40–2; G III, 199–200, 235).

Spinoza also appeals to history in support of the case against ecclesiastical authority, drawing specifically on the history of the Hebrew state. On his retelling, while the Hebrew state flourished under Moses' stewardship, it was undone when high priests seized political power in the second state. After acquiring power, these clerics "began to seek the glory of his own name both in religion and in other matters, determining everything by priestly authority and daily issuing new decrees, concerning ceremonies, the faith, and everything else, decrees they wanted to be no less sacred and to have no less authority than the laws of Moses" (TTP 18.8; G III, 222). The result of this was the eruption of irresolvable factional conflict.

Spinoza's account of the decline of the Hebrew commonwealth can be read as a very thinly veiled warning about the dangers of Calvinist fanaticism in the United Provinces. The decision to use the Hebrew state as an object lesson carried significant rhetorical force, as the history of the Israelites was woven into the self-conception of Dutch Calvinists as a chosen people. Spinoza is effectively saying *if you are going to model your identity on the Israelites, do not forget what brought about the destruction of their state.*

We see, then, that Spinoza gives theological, philosophical, and historical reasons for opposing clerical authority. But how does this add up to an argument for toleration? Putting civil authorities in charge of matters of religion looks like a restriction on religious liberty and a recipe for intolerance. However, Spinoza's claim is that civil authorities have full right to determine matters of faith – a claim known as Erastianism, after Swiss theologian Thomas Erastus (1524–1583) – and this contributes to toleration in that it undercuts the power of those whom he regards as most dangerous and intolerant: ambitious and superstitious religious leaders. By limiting their claim to power, Spinoza thinks he is disarming the greatest threat to freethinkers. It is also worth stressing that Spinoza's defense of toleration is primarily a defense of the freedom to philosophize, rather than a defense of freedom of religious practice. He is not especially concerned about the sovereign passing laws regulating the outward expression of faith; rather, he is worried that philosophical inquiry and discussion will be stifled by blasphemy laws. Still, the strongest arguments for toleration are contained in the concluding chapter of the work in which Spinoza advances arguments that are intended to restrict the reach of even the civil sovereign.

The secular case for toleration

Given that Spinoza thinks that a strong state is required to protect against ideological corruption, what justifies limiting the exercise of sovereign power in the way that Spinoza does? Why should a state not seek to overcome irrationality and bondage to the passions by coercive means, if necessary?

Spinoza has two types of response to this concern. The first is to argue that the sovereign lacks the power, and consequently the right, to control people's minds in this way. He writes that "no one can transfer to another person his natural right, *or* faculty, of reasoning freely, and of judging concerning anything whatever" (TTP 20.2; G III, 239). The state could only effectively regulate people's beliefs if it had the power to control them. And while Spinoza admits that one person may be able to dominate another's belief system in a multitude of ways, he also asserts that there are limits to just how much control can be exerted, for "men's minds differ as much as their palates do" (TTP 20.4; G III, 239). The state possesses at best a very limited right or power to compel belief.

Spinoza proceeds to argue that because people naturally express whatever they think, speech also lies beyond the scope of coercible activity:

> [N]o one can surrender his freedom of judging and thinking what he wishes, but everyone, by the greatest natural right, is master of his own thoughts, [from which] it follows that if the supreme powers in a republic try to make men say nothing but what they prescribe, no matter how different and contrary their opinions, they will get only the most unfortunate result. Not even the wisest know how to keep quiet, not to mention ordinary people. It's a common vice of men to confide their judgments to others, even if secrecy is needed. (TTP 20.8–9; G III, 240)

Thought and speech lie, at least to some extent, beyond the power or right of the sovereign.

But while Spinoza defends the freedoms of conscience and thought, he nevertheless insists that it *is* within the sovereign's ambit to regulate behavior.[21] At first blush, it might look like this distinction between thought and action presupposes a sharp split between the private mind and the public body, which Spinoza would regard as metaphysically dubious. If the mind and the body are one and the same thing considered in two different ways, then if the body can be controlled, so, it would seem, can the mind. In fact, Spinoza can account for the disparate treatment of thought and action without violating his metaphysics by acknowledging that there is a set of ideas that are more responsive to coercive pressure, namely, ideas about the utility of performing some action. The state may not be able to bring it about by law that one hates chocolate or believes that chocolate is evil, but it can make it so that one represents the activity of eating chocolate aversively by annexing penalties to such behavior.

The second set of reasons for limiting the scope of state interference is thoroughly prudential. Spinoza draws on his views about human psychology to argue that attempts to make people moral through legislation typically backfire: "Anyone who wants to limit everything by laws will provoke more vices than he'll correct" (TTP 20.24; G III, 243). Sumptuary laws, for instance, which aim to limit "extravagant living, envy, greed, drunkenness, and the like" (TTP 20.25; G III, 243), only foster these vices, feeding the very desires that the laws aim to restrain since we crave what we cannot have (TP 10/5). Spinoza also argues that people become defiant when their views are treated as vicious:

> For the most part men are so constituted that they endure nothing with greater impatience than that opinions they believe to be true should be considered criminal and that what moves them to piety toward God and men should be counted as wickedness in them. The result is that they dare to denounce the laws and do what they can against the magistrate; they don't think it shameful, but quite honorable, to initiate rebellions and attempt any crime for the sake of this cause. (TTP 20.29; G III, 244)

Outlawing forms of thought and expression only provokes resistance, which thereby weakens the state.

Finally, perhaps with a nod towards the history of *converso* Judaism, Spinoza notes that even if the state could successfully regulate expression, it could not do so without undermining the conditions under which trust and security are possible. If people were prohibited from expressing their sincere opinions, they "would think one thing and say something else. The result? The good faith especially necessary in a republic would be corrupted. Abominable flattery and treachery would be encouraged, as would deceptions and the corruption of the liberal studies" (TTP 20.27; G III, 243).[22]

Ultimately, trying to regulate belief and expression by law is counterproductive, destroying trust, promoting vice and resistance, and generally destabilizing the state. Conversely, by granting subjects the freedom to think and speak as they wish, they will more willingly and hopefully uphold the institutions of the state. Tolerant governance promotes affective buy-in, while enabling the arts and sciences to flourish (TTP 20.26; G III, 243).

But even if the freedom to philosophize really is, as Spinoza claims in the subtitle to the TTP, necessary for a peaceful, flourishing state, this leaves the scope of what is tolerated somewhat indeterminate. The state still has to make determinations about what counts as seditious speech and action, carefully weighing the potentially dangerous and destabilizing effects of the speech or behavior against the potentially destabilizing effects of legislative overreach. While some commentators have bemoaned the absence of a clearly delimited scope of civil liberties in Spinoza,[23] the admission that the scope of prudent tolerance is circumstance-relative might actually be one of its virtues.

Consider Spinoza's approach in relation to a salient challenge for liberals today, namely, how far one should tolerate hate speech, or speech that vilifies or degrades someone on the basis of their identity. Like religious bigotry, hate speech undermines peace by feeding the zeal of the ignorant and stigmatizing members of groups that are often already vulnerable and marginalized. On the other hand, there is some hope that, at least in a relatively enlightened society, permitting the expression of hate speech may strengthen the resolve of the citizenry in opposing bigotry. And, moreover, restricting speech may well have the consequence of making people who are accustomed to broad liberties more resentful towards government. So how far should a sovereign that wants to promote peace tolerate hate speech?

Spinoza would argue that to take a principled, once-and-for-all stance would be naive and imprudent. Instead, the state must weigh the harms wrought by its admission against the likelihood of resistance or backfire in the case of regulation. In countries where there is a dominant ethos of liberty – i.e., where people are accustomed to a very tolerant state with minimal intervention – the regulation of hate speech might be more destabilizing or disharmonizing than it would be in countries where there is a dominant ethos of fraternity. Accommodating the customs and psychological makeup of a particular people makes legislating rather complicated. But, given the complexity of the phenomena, perhaps a little messiness is to be expected.

7.5 Democratism

Whereas the main aim of the TTP is to defend the freedom of philosophizing, the main aim of the TP is to give an account of which institutions promote peace and rationality. The two treatises play complementary roles in Spinoza's normative political program: the

TTP seeks to protect the state from the noxious effects of clerical intolerance, while the TP advances a positive account of which institutions promote the civic aims of peace, security, and freedom. The recommendations for how to design institutions in the TP are made by way of an analysis of model regime forms. And while Spinoza died just as he began his analysis of a model democracy – leading one scholar to claim that "we watch him die before this blank page,"[24] as he confronted the problem of who counts as a citizen – the work as a whole can be seen as a defense of democratization, as even in the discussions of monarchy and aristocracy, the salient message throughout is that in order for such regimes to flourish, the power of the sovereign must be supported and checked by broad, participatory bodies, and that political decisions must be made in the open. States become more absolute – which is to say, more harmonious and more peaceful – as they approach a well-constituted democracy (TP 8/3, 11/1). As the work was written in the wake of the reestablishment of the stadtholdership in 1672, which marked the end of the pure republican period of the Dutch Republic, one way of understanding the work is as a kind of handbook for the stadtholder, with the main lesson being that in order for him (i.e., William III) to govern successfully and maintain his power, he must democratize the state.

In this section, we will examine why Spinoza thought that democratic institutions best promote peace and collective rationality. We will see that, as with his defense of toleration, Spinoza defends democratized institutions on the basis of pragmatic arguments grounded in his understanding of human psychology. Some of these arguments emphasize the way that democratic institutions promote affective buy-in or security in the sense discussed above; others emphasize the superior rationality of large deliberative bodies. Ultimately, the affective and the epistemic arguments for democracy emphasize different aspects of the same aim: peace, security, and freedom.

One of the main lines of argument from the TTP is that democracies best preserve our natural equality or liberty. For instance, Spinoza claims that in a democracy alone "no one is bound to be subject to his equal" (TTP 5.23; G III, 74) since one participates in one's own governance:

[O]bedience has no place in a social order where sovereignty is in the hands of everyone and laws are enacted by common consent, and [...] whether the laws in such a social order are increased or diminished, the people nevertheless remains equally free, because it does not act from the authority of someone else, but by its own consent. (TTP 5.25; G III, 74)

He makes a very similar claim later in the work, maintaining that democracies best preserve natural equality and natural freedom:

> I preferred to treat it [a democracy] before all others, because it seemed the most natural state, and the one which approached most nearly the freedom nature concedes to everyone. In it no one so transfers his natural right to another that in the future there is no consultation with him. Instead he transfers it to the greater part of the whole society, of which he makes one part. In this way everyone remains equal, as they were before, in the state of nature. (TTP 16.36; G III, 195)[25]

Appeals to natural liberty and equality in defense of popular governance were a mainstay of early-modern republican thought. One finds similar claims in the writings of Machiavelli, Pieter de la Court, and Algernon Sidney. What is somewhat distinctive about Spinoza's views is that he does not claim as Sidney does, for instance, that dependency on the decisions of another is bad per se. Rather, Spinoza asserts that subordination is unstable since the "hardest thing for [people] to endure is being subservient to their equals, and being governed by them" (TTP 5.22; G III, 74). Just as we resist illiberal governance, we resist subordination to perceived equals. In the TP in particular, Spinoza stresses that static hierarchical relations breed envy, hatred, and resistance, and thereby undermine civic unity (TP 7/13). Conversely, by allowing for broad participation in the formation of the sovereign will and rendering political posts available to all, democracies foster greater trust and a more stable state (TP 7/2), marked by a more willing, more secure citizenry.

In addition to the claim that democracies breed security and harmony, Spinoza also advances a series of epistemic arguments in defense of democratic institutions. Otherwise put, he claims that democratized states will tend to make better collective judgments than less democratized alternatives. One reason for this is that large, deliberative bodies bring new information and new perspectives to light. In one particularly inspired, if somewhat overblown, passage, Spinoza writes that "human wits are too sluggish to penetrate everything right away. But by asking advice, listening, and arguing, they're sharpened. When people try all means, in the end they find ways to the things they want which everyone approves, and no one had ever thought of before" (TP 9/14). Even if deliberative decision-making bodies are somewhat inefficient, this downside is more than offset by the improvement in the quality of decisions that follow vigorous debate. The larger the deliberative body, the better, since "[i]f the assembly is large, it's almost impossible that the majority of its members should agree on one absurd action" (TTP 16.30; G III, 194). The guiding assumption in these passages is that after exposure to a wide range of views, members of a large deliberative group are likely to avoid making very bad decisions and may well converge on good ones.

Deliberation also helps to rein in the pursuit of private interest. In regimes where the power of governing agents is unchecked, the ruling class will tend to legislate self-servingly, at the cost of the general good: "[W]hen the few decide everything, simply on the basis of their own affects, freedom and the common good are lost" (TP 9/14).[26] Democratic accountability helps to keep in check what he calls in the TTP the "absurdities of appetite" (TTP 16.30; G III, 194), in part because participants must invoke broad, civic reasons for one's position (TP 8/6).

Perhaps most importantly, democratized institutions promote the "balancing of interests," aligning individual desires with public goods (TTP 17.16 [G III, 203], TP 6/3, 7/2). This requires that political power be broadly distributed. For instance, in a democratized, balanced monarchy, the monarch will be compelled to make judgments based on the advice of a large, incorruptible body of citizen counselors (TP 7/3, 7/9, 8/38), whose "personal situation and advantage" are made to "depend on peace and the common well-being of everyone" (TP 7/4). Such accountability mechanisms include periodic elections, term limits, the rotation of offices, and the adoption of regulatory councils, which help to limit individual power and ensure that individual or factional interests are not advanced at the expense of the general good. States that lack these institutions and concentrate power too narrowly are easily toppled. This is how Spinoza explains the fall of De Witt's republic,[27] which was content to retain the old institutions except for the stadtholder, creating a situation in which "those who really had the authority were *far too few* to be able to govern the multitude and overcome powerful opponents" (TP 9/14, emphasis added).

To appreciate that these are epistemic arguments, one must bear in mind once again that reason and the emotions are inextricably connected for Spinoza. Reliable control over one's wayward passions is evidence of rationality; and the lack of appetitive control is evidence of irrationality. As a slogan: the conative expresses the cognitive. This thesis applies at the state level. To the extent that the state is moved to act by desires that undermine its own ability to exist and act (i.e., its own power), it is irrational. So, when some part of the body politic advances a private interest at the expense of the general good, even if its members in some sense know what would be good for the state as a whole, the state is acting irrationally. Hence while aristocracies might be wise in theory, "experience has shown abundantly that [...] the will of the patricians is least bound by the law, because they lack rivals. For there the patricians, in a partisan spirit, keep the best men off the council, and seek comrades on it who will hang on their every word" (TP 11/2). A knowledgeable, but unconstrained, elite will typically exhibit worse collective judgment than a democracy because the former is more susceptible to the absurdities of appetite. By claiming that democracies tend to exhibit greater appetitive control than other regimes, Spinoza upends the Platonic order, according to which democracies are dominated by the appetites. Spinoza invokes the pervasive self-interest of individuals in support of democratic government, provided that strong accountability mechanisms are in place.

This last observation leads to a crucial qualification regarding Spinoza's defense of democracy, which is that certain conditions need to obtain in order for democracies to be successful. For instance, in order for deliberation to "sharpen the wits" of the participants and converge on rational decisions, deliberative bodies must be free from the influence of fearmongering, superstitious clerics. This is why he organizes the TTP around preventing or counteracting this form of state corruption. The danger of mob mentality would have impressed itself upon Spinoza in the brutal slayings of the De Witts in 1672. So, when Spinoza claims that in a large, deliberative body, the majority is unlikely to make irrational judgments, this would seem to be conditional on the establishment of reasonably good epistemic conditions.

Spinoza stresses the importance of good epistemic conditions forcefully near the end of TP chapter 7, where he attempts to rebut those who claim that common people are too stupid and tempestuous to participate in governance. Spinoza is at his most fiercely anti-elitist in these passages (TP 7/27–9): "[E]veryone shares a common nature – we're just deceived by power and culture" (TP 7/27, translation modified). Widespread differences between people's capacities can be ultimately traced back to divergent civil structures and practices. One particularly important factor that he cites here is access to information. The main reason that most people are poor judges in political matters is that governors tend to operate in secrecy:

> [I]t's no surprise that "there's neither truth nor judgment in the plebeians" when the rulers manage the chief business of the state secretly, and the plebeians are only making a guess from the few things the rulers can't conceal. [...] So it's sheer stupidity to want to do everything in secrecy, and then expect the citizens not to judge the government's actions wrongly, and not to interpret everything perversely. (TP 7/27)

Spinoza follows this with a plea for political transparency: "[I]t's much better for the state's proper and true plans to be open to its enemies than for a tyrant's wicked secrets to be kept from his citizens" (TP 7/29). Without adequate access to information, the people cannot effectively deliberate or hold their leaders accountable, and the epistemic advantage of popular participation in governance will be lost. But if the state promotes broad political engagement and governs transparently, we can reasonably expect widespread competency since everyone is "shrewd and clever enough in matters he has long been passionately involved in" (TP 7/4).

There are, thus, at least two sets of conditions that must obtain in order for democracies to function well: the state must be free from ideological contamination (e.g., from religious clerics) and it must be governed openly, before the vigilant eyes of an engaged citizenry. In light of these observations about the need for good epistemic conditions, we see that Spinoza's arguments point to the potential virtues of democracies while also indicating how vulnerable they are to corruption. His democratism is at once promising and sobering. Large, deliberative bodies that govern transparently and are not under the spell of clerical zealots are likely to make better judgments than other governing bodies. However, in the absence of such good cognitive conditions, the masses may well be reduced to a muddled mob.

7.6 Liberation and the state

We opened this chapter by asking why Spinoza would devote so much energy in the last decade of his life to writing about politics

– the realm of action and corruption – given his lofty vision of freedom in the *Ethics* as perfecting the intellect. We have seen, though, that, for Spinoza, politics aims at the very same thing that moral philosophy does: liberation or empowerment. And the state can contribute to intellectual perfection in a variety of ways: by dismantling institutions that promote superstition and persecution; by adopting a policy of toleration, so that philosophy and freethinking can flourish; by promoting passions like hope and love rather than obstacles to knowledge like fear and envy; and by designing institutions that encourage deliberation and facilitate the dissemination of knowledge. Moreover, as we become more secure and more powerful through our engagement with others, adversarial and competitive stances give way to a more cooperative stance whereby we recognize the extent to which our power and welfare is bound up with the power and welfare of others and with the success of the commonwealth as a whole. Perhaps it is only through living in a peaceful, harmonious state that we can fully come to appreciate the dictum from the *Ethics* that "man is a God to man" (4p35). The political works reveal the extent to which, according to Spinoza, one's individual flourishing is bound up with the flourishing of the collective.

Further reading

Balibar, Étienne. 1998. *Spinoza and Politics*, trans. by Peter Snowdon. London: Verso.

James, Susan. 2012. *Spinoza on Philosophy, Religion, and Politics:* The Theologico-Political Treatise. Oxford: Oxford University Press, chs 10–12.

Melamed, Yitzhak Y. and Rosenthal, Michael A. (eds). 2010. *Spinoza's* Theological-Political Treatise: *A Critical Guide*. Cambridge: Cambridge University Press.

Sharp, Hasana. 2011. *Spinoza and the Politics of Renaturalization*. Chicago: University of Chicago Press.

Sharp, Hasana and Melamed, Yitzhak Y. (eds). 2018. *Spinoza's* Political Treatise: *A Critical Guide*. Cambridge: Cambridge University Press.

Steinberg, Justin. 2018. *Spinoza's Political Psychology: The Taming of Fortune and Fear*. Cambridge: Cambridge University Press.

8

Spinoza's Reception

As we noted in the opening chapter, Spinoza's reputation as a reclusive thinker is ill-founded: he had a relatively wide circle of friends who eagerly studied his philosophy while it was in the making, and his burial attracted a great many mourners. Of course, there were no shortage of adversaries either; but the commotion caused by the TTP ensured that there was never any danger that his work would fall into oblivion. In fact, Spinoza's posthumous reception is a saga unto itself, full of dramatic twists and turns. For the sake of simplicity, we divide that reception into three periods.[1]

8.1 The tumultuous first century

After Spinoza's death, his friends prepared both Latin and Dutch editions of his corpus astonishingly quickly. This was a remarkable editorial feat, especially given that they were forced to work under hazardous conditions: for months, the essential body of Spinoza's philosophical legacy existed only as manuscripts, located in Jan Rieuwertsz's publishing house while ecclesiastical authorities were looking for them. Fortunately, already by the end of 1677, both the *Opera Posthuma* and *De nagelate schriften* were completed, appearing in the beginning of 1678 and containing also the unfinished *Treatise on the Emendation of the Intellect* and the *Political Treatise*. The front page of both Latin and Dutch editions include only the initials of the author, "B. d. S." and the year 1677; neither the publisher nor the place of publication are mentioned. The importance of the *Opera*

Posthuma notwithstanding, for a long time the TTP was considerably more extensively disseminated than the *Ethics*. Moreover, unlike the *Ethics*, which appeared in (non-Dutch) vernacular quite late – in 1744 in German, in 1842 in French, and only in 1883 in English – the TTP appeared already in 1678 in French, in 1689 in English, and in 1693 in Dutch.

Unsurprisingly, during the final decades of the seventeenth and the first half of the eighteenth century the reaction to Spinoza's thought as a whole was predominantly hostile: he was widely claimed to be an atheist, materialist, and fatalist of the worst kind. Emblematically, even the Dutch Republic rushed to ban all of Spinoza's philosophy right after the publication of his posthumous works. Although Spinoza himself had consistently denied being an atheist – after all, all he does is talk of God – there are solid reasons for the dangerous reputation. Nobody before him – and nobody long, if ever, after him – had developed as thoroughgoing a critique of the traditional Judeo-Christian worldview.[2] Although there were plenty of thinkers sharing and distributing heterodox ideas even if one were not willing to grant to Spinoza such a colossal influence on the early modern Europe as Jonathan Israel famously does,[3] it is unquestionably true that Spinoza provided a singularly systematic, tightly argued, and multifaceted attack on the prevailing political, philosophical, and religious establishment. As we have seen, he espouses an unqualified naturalism that identifies God with all of nature, denies providence and the freedom of will, and claims that everything takes place necessarily, as dictated by laws of nature. Still, it was Spinoza's biblical criticism that prompted the greatest furor, along with his categorical denial of miracles, defense of toleration for all philosophy, and criticism of ecclesiastical authority.[4]

Indeed, Spinoza came to be the epitome of Enlightenment, radical in the sense that instead of being concerned about reconciling faith and philosophy, as more moderate thinkers were, he considers religion to be in an important sense inferior to philosophy and reduces the message of Scripture to a few practical principles beneficial for social coexistence.[5] As a consequence, it did not take long for "Spinozism" to become a veritable brand with a reputation nasty enough to be used as a cudgel with which to assail thinkers not willing to comply with the prevailing religious orthodoxy. Spinoza's name abounds in pamphlets, letters, and books denouncing "freethinkers" and "unbelievers." In fact, charges of Spinozism were at times quite arbitrarily wielded also against certain Christians (such as rational theologians Jean Le Clerc and John Locke) simply because one found something offensive in their views. Also, philosophers joined their forces and treated Spinoza at least until the mid-eighteenth century, to borrow Lessing's words, "like a dead dog," a public denunciation of Spinozism often being a routine procedure before obtaining one's professorship. To put the record straight, catalogues of anti-Spinozists were compiled in eighteenth-century Germany, listing hundreds of clerics and philosophers for having valiantly lambasted Spinozism. Then again, all the opposition had, at least to some extent, the ironic effect of making Spinoza's thought more widely known than it would otherwise have been; in fact, some of his persecutors realized this and, at least some time after his death, tried to avoid mentioning Spinoza by name.

Still, Spinoza and Spinozism also had allies. Most notably, there were those who came from Cartesian and heterodox Christian backgrounds and identified themselves as freethinkers and even Spinozists; people such as Jarig Jellesz, Lodewijk Meyer, Georg Hermann Schuller, and Jan Hendrik Glazemaker, who were also responsible for the publication of Spinoza's posthumous works. Unsurprisingly, given not only that Spinoza had lived in the country but also that the first vernacular version of his works appeared in Dutch, the first group of this type appeared in the Netherlands and remained a force to be reckoned until the 1720s. However, despite the efforts of the authorities, Spinoza's ideas kept spreading subterraneously in the neighboring countries in manuscript form and mixed with doctrines derived from other clandestine thinkers. The best-known and by far most widely circulated was the *Traité des trois imposteurs* (or *La vie et l'esprit de Mr. Benoît de Spinoza*), the author of which is a matter of dispute. After having existed for years as manuscripts, it was finally published in 1719. This text was based on a rather crude exposition of Spinozistic tenets, onto which some other heterodox ideas were grafted. It was translated into Latin, German, English, and Italian. Fierce and indignant in its tone, *Traité des trois imposteurs* served as a blunt but no doubt effective vehicle for propagating ideas denying fundamental Judeo-Christian tenets. Little by little, Spinoza's ideas infiltrated basically all of Europe. In France, they had a clear influence on the most damned of the materialists, Julien Offray de La Mettrie (1709–1751), the author of *L'Homme Machine* (1748), and on the monistic vitalism developed by Denis Diderot (1713–1784).[6] In the British Isles, Spinoza's influence was not as strong, and his thought was often associated with that of Hobbes; the most prominent figure is the Irish philosopher John

Toland (1670–1722), generally considered a Spinozist. Toland established the term "pantheism," with which Spinoza's thought is still most often characterized.

It can thus generally be said that Spinoza's influence crossed theological as well as geographical boundaries. Still, a surprising bloc of Spinozistically minded people deserve a special mention for their later influence: German Lutherans, disenchanted with the fact that the Lutheran Church had become part of the establishment, endangering if not rejecting such pivotal Lutheran ideas as a priesthood of all believers and freedom of religious conscience. The idea that we have a direct individual experience and relationship to (the pantheistically understood) God was especially crucial in turning them towards key Spinozistic tenets.

All in all, the century following Spinoza's death was a peculiar era: individuals maintained dual (or multiple) intellectual identities, sometimes shrouding their most subversive opinions in cloaks of respectability, manuscripts with fictitious titles were circulated underground, and freethinkers were often persecuted for obscure reasons. There is probably no better representative of this period than Pierre Bayle (1647–1706), whose *Dictionnaire historique et critique* (1697/1702) might have been the most read work of the early Enlightenment. The most extensive entry in the magnum opus of this immensely learned scholar, outwardly a loyal member of the Reformed Church of the Netherlands, is on Spinoza. Bayle had studied Spinoza for decades and already in 1682 designated him as the model of a *virtuous atheist* – a characterization that once appeared oxymoronic. In the *Dictionnaire*, Bayle presents a famous set of objections to Spinoza, some of which are still occasionally brought up in the scholarship. But many of his arguments fail miserably enough to have made readers doubt whether they are sincere or whether his real intention was to disseminate Spinozistic ideas. This is in line with the fact that Bayle's philosophico-theological convictions were, and still are, something of a mystery: it is a matter of controversy whether he was an honest but heterodox Christian, a disguised antireligious radical, or something in between, such as a skeptic of an indiscernible ilk.

It has been questioned to what extent invocations of "Spinoza" or "Spinozism" referred to anything like the actual Spinoza and his thought. In light of the preceding discussion, it is clear that most parties involved had not really studied Spinoza's works – the slow appearance of the *Ethics* in vernacular being one hindrance to firsthand study– and that Spinoza's reputation grew via clandestine manuscripts compiled in the heated atmosphere of the era. However, it does not follow from this that the prevalent conception of Spinoza's core theses would have been seriously erroneous. After all, it is not that difficult to understand, at least in their broad outlines, such claims as that there is no anthropomorphic, providential, and transcendent God but only one substance, the whole of Nature, of which we are part; that there are neither miracles nor free will, only laws of nature; that the Bible is the historical artifact of numerous unknown authors; and that all thought, no matter how outrageous, should be freely tolerated. All of these ideas were widely, and correctly, attributed to Spinoza.

8.2 The long nineteenth century: the rise to fame

Rarely, if ever, has a thinker's reputation transformed as abruptly as Spinoza's did in the 1780s. The so-called pantheism controversy (*Pantheismusstreit*) of 1785 turned him almost overnight from a villain to a hero. The controversy involved three German intellectual luminaries: G. E. Lessing (1729–1781), Moses Mendelssohn (1729–1786), and F. H. Jacobi (1743–1819). In its broad outlines, the story goes as follows. Lessing and Mendelssohn were regarded as among the most revered figures of the German Enlightenment; after Lessing died, Mendelssohn planned to write a book on his departed friend. However, in 1783, Jacobi – an unremitting critic of Enlightenment rationalism – wrote to Mendelssohn that in the summer of 1780 he had visited Lessing. Much to Jacobi's amazement, Lessing had confessed that he was a Spinozist, believing in the pantheist credo *hen kai pan*, "one and all," and denying that there are final causes, free will, providence, or a personal God. Mendelssohn did not directly deny the authenticity of this report but tried to preempt the shockwave of Lessing's confession by starting to write a book, *Morgenstunden*, in which to present his own version of Lessing's confession: that it was, at most, a sign of endorsing what Mendelssohn called "purified pantheism," which admits that all things inhere in God's intellect but denies that God is extended or without intellect and will – making Lessing's God resemble that of Leibniz and Wolff. Jacobi, however, got to know about Mendelssohn's plans, and both men hurried to be the first to publish his version of the issue. Jacobi won that race: in 1785, his quickly compiled *Über die Lehre des Spinoza in Briefen an den Herrn Moses Mendelssohn* was published a month before *Morgenstunden*.

This prompted Mendelssohn to write a refutation of Jacobi entitled *An die Freunde Lessings*, in which he claimed that Jacobi had been fooled by Lessing's penchant for dialectical skirmishes filled with paradoxes and that any of his putative confessions were thus not to be taken seriously. However, the cat was already out of the bag, the news of Lessing's Spinozism having hit the public consciousness. After having hastily delivered his final manuscript of *An die Freunde Lessings*, on a cold winter's day, to the publisher, Mendelssohn fell ill and died a few days later, on January 4, 1786. This unexpected and sad ending to the controversy made it a scandal, with many of Mendelssohn's friends accusing Jacobi of killing him.

The seemingly abrupt controversy did not appear from thin air. Lessing belonged precisely to the aforementioned pantheistic Lutherans, and he had studied Spinoza since 1763, the very year when Jacobi also discovered Spinoza. Thus by 1780, both had done their homework on Spinoza, drawing very different conclusions from what they had learned. Mendelssohn, the prime representative of the moderate Wolffian Enlightenment, knew Spinoza's work well too. His *Philosophische Gespräche* of 1755 is a pioneering attempt to present Spinoza in an impartial and even sympathetic fashion. This is in line with the fact that despite all the persecution and efforts to abolish Spinozism, by 1785 Spinoza had made such an impact in Germany that there were a notable number of crypto-Spinozists ready to be open about their convictions. If a thinker of Lessing's stature, reputation, and judgment was a Spinozist, there was no shame in being one. Jacobi's intention was to show, via Lessing's example, that Spinozistic naturalism leads to fatalism, atheism, and – the word he made known to modern philosophy – nihilism. Mendelssohn, on the other hand, was concerned that Lessing's reputation would become tarnished. Both were proved wrong, and something unexpected happened: the controversy had the unintended effect of making Spinozism a kind of intellectual fashion. In fact, it came to be seen as the only viable competitor to increasingly popular Kantianism. Spinoza's naturalism was widely deemed as the philosophy proper of the scientific worldview, whereas his pantheism was interpreted in the religious register. The Romantic poet Novalis (1772–1801) famously praised him as "the God-intoxicated man [*der Gott betrunkene Mensch*]." As a consequence, Spinozism appeared, of all things, a welcome middle path between obsolete theism and straightforward atheism – an astonishing turn of events for a philosophy once condemned as heinously sacrilegious.

The ensuing German interest in Spinoza is so multifarious that we can only very superficially survey it. Still, one work deserves a special mention: Johann Gottfried Herder's (1744–1803) *Gott: Einige Gespräche* of 1787. This book, which presents a bold and enthusiastic interpretation of Spinoza's philosophy, had a major influence on how Spinoza was received in the aftermath of the pantheism controversy. Herder embraces Spinoza as an ingenious and profound thinker constrained by the obsolete view of the science of his era; as the eighteenth century had progressed, for instance, biology, physics, and chemistry had shown that the mechanical sciences were unable to explain such phenomena as magnetism, electricity, gravitation, and living organisms – a new paradigm was needed. That paradigm, for Herder as for many other thinkers, was vitalism, and Herder saw nothing problematic in combining Spinoza's system with it. This means that Herder adopts Spinoza's monism – emphasizing the fact that it is a form of pantheism, not atheism – and sees Spinoza's substance as a primal *force* that results in organisms endowed with living forces. Moreover, and more controversially, building on the fact that necessitarianism need not entail the denial of final causes, Herder claims that a pantheistic God can have understanding and will, and can thus act intentionally. This, in turn, is supposed to keep the specter of fatalism at bay.

Due to these developments, Spinoza's philosophy was approached in an entirely new fashion: his naturalism was seen as the apogee of scientific rationalism, and his pantheistic monism inspired, in various ways, the major German Romantics and Idealists of the post-Kantian era. Some sought to incorporate aspects of Spinozism into their thought. For instance, J. W. Goethe (1749–1832) endeavored to conduct his botanical studies according to the model provided by Spinoza's – his favorite philosopher's – third kind of knowledge. But many others saw Spinozism as a formidable challenge to be *overcome* – especially after Immanuel Kant's (1724–1804) subjectivity-emphasizing first *Critique* – as the philosophy "of the object."[7] To mention probably the two most notable thinkers in this regard, the whole philosophical career of F. W. J. Schelling (1775–1854), who was a key philosopher of the Romantic era, revolved to a notable extent around Spinoza – perhaps most prominently in Schelling's philosophy of nature. Slightly later, G. W. F. Hegel (1770–1831) contended that either one endorses Spinoza's thought or has no philosophy at all; but for him, Spinozism – which Hegel saw as acosmism, or the denial of the reality of finite existents

– is nevertheless just the beginning of philosophy, to be superseded by absolute idealism. Indeed, Spinoza's system has relatively often – and one-dimensionally – been seen as a form of materialism and thus at odds with Hegelianism.

In general, it may perhaps be said that the post-Hegelian era represents a kind of a *normalization* period in Spinoza's reception. The nineteenth century brought metaphysics back in a way that made discussing Spinoza's views quite natural. Accordingly, a notable critical edition of Spinoza's works appeared in 1882–1883, edited by Johannes van Vloten and J. P. N. Land, and what may probably be called the first school of Spinoza interpretation emerged when such British Idealists as John Caird (1820–1898), James Martineau (1805–1900), Frederick Pollock (1845–1937), and Harold H. Joachim (1868–1938) wrote treatises on Spinoza, arguing that he is forced to a position according to which thought is the only attribute and finite things are illusory. More generally, the times had changed: Arthur Schopenhauer (1788–1860), according to whom this world is a miserable place of endless suffering, became a virtual superstar in the 1860s, which resulted in a notable number of pessimistic philosophers who took Spinoza into account without the emotional burden of the past. In the 1880s, Friedrich Nietzsche (1844–1900) in turn declared that God is dead and that it is humans who killed him. In this kind of philosophical climate, even though Spinoza was still often criticized, his thought simply could not have the kind of shock value it formerly had.

8.3 Spinoza until today: the silent years and the scholarly renaissance

Compared to all the commotion that had taken place thus far, the first half of the twentieth century marked a notably peaceful period in Spinoza's reception. On the one hand, as noted, the zeitgeist had changed so that his thought could not give rise to the kind of agitation it formerly had. On the other hand, the two dominant philosophical factions, analytic philosophy in the anglophone world and phenomenology on the continent, had little interest in the grand metaphysical systems of Spinoza's variety. The critical edition of Spinoza's *oeuvre* still in use, edited by Carl Gebhardt and published in 1925, was the most significant scholarly achievement of this era. This does not mean that Spinoza would not have been studied during the opening decades of the century; there were, to name just a few, such notable scholars as Léon Brunschvicq (1869–1944) in France, Stanislaus von Dunin-Borkowski (1864–1934) in Germany, the aforementioned Harold H. Joachim in England, and Harry A. Wolfson (1887–1974) in the United States.

Although Spinoza was never forgotten, it was still not until the 1960s that a veritable boom in Spinoza studies began to emerge. This was especially true in France: Martial Gueroult published two hugely influential tomes on the first two parts of the *Ethics* in 1968 and 1974, with two other classic studies appearing almost simultaneously, namely Gilles Deleuze's *Spinoza et le problème de l'expression* in 1968 and Alexandre Matheron's *Individu et communauté chez Spinoza* only a year later.[8] Meanwhile in the anglophone world, a new era in Spinoza studies was ushered in by Stuart Hampshire's *Spinoza* (1951), furthered by Edwin Curley's *Spinoza's Metaphysics* (1969), and cemented by Jonathan Bennett's influential and critical *A Study of Spinoza's* Ethics (1984).

Ever since then, scholarly interest in Spinoza has shown no signs of waning, with for instance Michael Della Rocca's, Don Garrett's, Chantal Jaquet's, Pierre-François Moreau's, and Piet Steenbakkers's work in the 1990s paving the way to the new millennium, with Steven Nadler's authoritative biography ending the decade.[9] Spinoza's political philosophy used to receive considerably more interest on the continent than in anglophone countries, in which he has been traditionally approached first and foremost as a rationalist metaphysician; but due to the influence of Étienne Balibar and contributions by such specialists as Susan James and Theo Verbeek, things have changed also in this respect. Indeed, the past twenty years have witnessed a global renaissance of Spinoza scholarship: there is hardly an aspect of his works that has not been extensively studied. Moreover, a new critical edition of Spinoza's *oeuvre*, intended to supersede the Gebhardt edition, is in the making in France under Moreau's editorship, and the second volume of the most widely used English translation, by Curley, appeared in 2016.[10] All in all, there can be little doubt that Spinoza's philosophy now enjoys the esteem that his personality always did, and he is for good reason widely celebrated as one of the most fascinating and formidable figures in western thought.

Further reading

Förster, Eckart and Melamed, Yitzhak Y. (eds). 2012. *Spinoza and German Idealism*. Cambridge: Cambridge University Press.

Israel, Jonathan. 2001. *Radical Enlightenment: Philosophy and the Making of Modernity 1650–1750*. Oxford: Oxford University Press.

Moreau, Pierre-François and Lærke, Mogens. Forthcoming. "Spinoza's Reception," in Don Garrett (ed.), *The Cambridge Companion to Spinoza*, 2nd edn. Cambridge: Cambridge University Press.

Van Bunge, Wiep. 2012. *Spinoza Past and Present: Essays on Spinoza, Spinozism, and Spinoza Scholarship*. Leiden: Brill.

Notes

Chapter 1 Spinoza's Life

1 The relatively brief sketch of Spinoza's life presented in this chapter is indebted to several informative biographical studies, including Curley 1985; Nadler 1999; Klever 1996; and Yovel 1989.
2 One commentator has, somewhat hyperbolically, called Van den Enden "the genius behind Spinoza," claiming that Van den Enden's writings "contain a political theory which is in fact the same as the one worked out by Spinoza" (Klever 1996: 26).
3 For the full list of abbreviations, see the section "Primary Sources and Abbreviations," pp. viii–ix.
4 Cited in Klever 1996: 34–5.
5 Aubrey 1898, I: 357.
6 Russell 1945: 569.

Chapter 2 Reality as God or Nature

1 Ontology is the study of the general nature of being, or the most basic features of what exists; as such, it is something found already in Aristotle in his discussion of "being as being" (see, e.g., *Metaphysics* IV; CWA I, 42–4).
2 Parts of this chapter are adapted from Viljanen 2009.
3 Aristotle's *Categories* (1a16–3b23; CWA II, 3–6) is here the most important original source; but also *Metaphysics* 1017b10–25 (CWA I, 68–9) should be noted. See also Carriero 1995.
4 See, e.g., *Principles* I.56; CSM I, 211–12.
5 For an example of this, see note 8 below.
6 In addition, there is the issue concerning how to interpret the concept of attribute, to which we will turn in the next section.
7 For a thorough analysis of this, see Carriero 1995: 248–50.

8 A pivotal element in Descartes's approach that we have not been able to locate in any of his predecessors is the idea that *there are only two basic properties*, of which other properties are modifications and through which those other properties are conceived.

9 See also Carriero 1995; D. Steinberg 2000: ch. 2.

10 Clearly, there is a close connection between inherence and conception. As Don Garrett (1990b: 107) puts it, Spinoza's way of deducing the claim that there is nothing apart from substances and modes "suggests that Spinoza understands 'a is in b' and 'a is conceived through b' as mutually entailing, either through their own meaning, or through the mediation of one or more axioms."

11 Bennett 1984: 61.

12 It should be noted that Spinoza himself does not accept this traditional definition (see especially 2p40s1, but also CM I.1; G I, 235).

13 See Gueroult 1968: 47–50; Curley 1969: ch. 1.

14 Much of the debate concerning the status of attributes has revolved around the fact that the Latin term *tanquam* in 1def4 can be translated both as "as" and "as if" ("as if" would arguably speak for the subjectivist interpretation); see, e.g., Shein 2009.

15 See, e.g., 1p9, 1p19, 1p20d. Gueroult (1968: 50) presents the classic, and according to some conclusive, objection to the subjectivist interpretation: the perceiving subject can only be a mere mode, which would make substances dependent on modes in a way that would violate Spinoza's most fundamental ontological priorities.

16 It should, however, be noted that Spinoza makes it rather clear in Ep. 56 (to Hugo Boxel) that there are more attributes than the two with which we are familiar.

17 The argument itself comes from, again, Della Rocca (2002: 17–22).

18 "Man thinks" (2a2) is an axiom in the *Ethics*, so there seems to be a path open to a *cogito* argument for the existence of the thinking subject. However, Spinoza makes no move to take it.

19 Here we are basically explicating what Spinoza writes in 1p6d2.

20 The longer route goes via 1p5: because substances cannot share an attribute (1p5), they do not have anything in common (1p2) and so (by 1p3) one cannot be the cause of the other; because the only external thing that could produce a substance is another substance (from 1def3, 1def5, and 1a1), a substance cannot be produced by anything else. It should be noted that also 1p3d invokes 1a4.

21 We should keep in mind the context in which Spinoza finds invoking the principle of sufficient reason appropriate: when trying to find out *the reason why something exists or not*.

22 This generates the thorny problem – discussing of which is beyond this chapter – of on what grounds can Spinoza claim that only one God with an infinity of attributes exists, rather than many substances with, say, one attribute. For a detailed discussion of this, see Garrett 1979.

23 See, e.g, Viljanen 2011: ch. 2; Hübner 2015.
24 See also Carriero 1995; Garrett 2002; Della Rocca 2008: ch. 2.
25 As far as we can see, Spinoza uses these two terms interchangeably.
26 It should be noted that in addition to such quotidian finite modes as
    trees and rocks there are also modes Spinoza calls *infinite* (1p21–p23),
    such as *motion and rest* in extension (Ep. 64; G IV, 278). However, their
    nature and function has been notoriously difficult to discern; see, e.g.,
    Melamed 2013: ch. 4.
27 A famous proposition sheds some light on how God's properties as
    modes produce, and stand in causal relationship with, each other:
    "Every singular thing, *or* any thing which is finite and has a determinate
    existence, can neither exist nor be determined to produce an effect unless
    it is determined to exist and produce an effect by another cause, which is
    also finite and has a determinate existence; and again, this cause also can
    neither exist nor be determined to produce an effect unless it is deter-
    mined to exist and produce an effect by another, which is also finite and
    has a determinate existence, and so on, to infinity" (1p28). Still, modes
    can also be at least to a certain extent intrinsically – that is, actively –
    determined (2p29s), which is fundamental for Spinoza's philosophy of
    action and moral philosophy; see sections 5.2, 5.5, 6.2, and 6.4.
28 See Garrett 1991 and Jarrett 2009; for a differing view, Curley and
    Walski 1999.

Chapter 3 Religion

 1 See *Summa contra Gentiles* I.72–4.
 2 *Reportatio* III, q. 12; cited in Haldane 1989: 43.
 3 The Fifth Meditation (CSM II, 44–5).
 4 See section 2.4.
 5 For more on this, see section 4.5.
 6 See, e.g., 1app, 1p32c1–2.
 7 See 1def7.
 8 See also section 6.4.
 9 In section 6.2.
10 He maintains that those who endorse voluntarism are "nearer to the
    truth than […] those who maintain that God does all things for the sake
    of the good" (1p33s2).
11 See also 2p3s, Ep. 56.
12 See section 7.4.
13 https://legacy.fordham.edu/halsall/mod/1562belgicconfession.asp
    (accessed in March 2020).
14 Israel 1995: 452–4.
15 Parts of this section are adapted from J. Steinberg 2018a: ch. 6.
16 See section 4.3.

17 Cf. 2p16c2.
18 See, e.g., TTP 14.9; G III, 174.
19 For more on Spinoza's views of toleration, see section 7.4.

Chapter 4 Knowledge and the Human Mind

1 On infinite modes, see chapter 2, note 26.
2 As noted in chapter 2 (note 16), although we are acquainted only with two attributes, thought and extension, Spinoza seems to think that there are infinitely many attributes; in line with this, the beginning of the second part of the *Ethics* leaves the scope of the objects of God's ideas completely open, not restricting them to things that fall under the two attributes familiar to us.
3 Recall section 2.1.
4 This claim has been the topic of debate ever since its introduction; for Arnauld's classic criticism, see the Fourth Set of Objections (CSM II, 139–44); for Descartes's replies, see the Fourth Set of Replies (CSM II, 154–62).
5 For discussion on mind and body in the *Meditations*, see, e.g., Broughton 2002: ch. 7; Carriero 2009: ch. 2.
6 For more on this, see Simmons 2017.
7 This is presented by Daniel Garber (2001: 173–4).
8 For discussion on the Cartesian mind–body union, see Cottingham 1986: ch. 5; Hoffman 1986; Alanen 2003: ch. 2; Brown 2006: ch. 5.
9 This is not to say that Spinoza would not acknowledge the experiential awareness we have of our embodiment: "We feel that a certain body is affected in many ways" (2a4).
10 See section 2.2.
11 Recall that modes are ontologically posterior to and dependent on their attributes.
12 Cf. 1def2.
13 Spinoza elaborates his view, again in a decidedly geometrical manner, in the next proposition (2p8); however, discussing it would take us too far afield. For a recent interpretation of that proposition, see Viljanen 2018.
14 As 2a4 (see note 9 above) displays, Spinoza is rather unmoved by sceptical considerations also with regard to the mind–body relationship; on Spinoza's generally depreciative attitude toward scepticism, see Viljanen 2020.
15 See 2p6, 2p13, 3p2.
16 See the next section and chapters 5–6.
17 See Nadler 2008.
18 Also the *Short Treatise* (II.2; G I, 55–6) treats knowledge, albeit very briefly.

19 More precisely, since Peter's body is an individual that consists of innumerable smaller bodies (2p15), Peter's perception of the horse is first and foremost about *the part* of Peter's body directly affected by the body of the horse.

20 See also 2p32.

21 Della Rocca 1996 forms the starting point of an especially lively discussion on this topic.

22 For a more detailed discussion defending this position, see Viljanen 2020.

23 For a helpful discussion of common notions, see Marshall 2013: ch. 2.

24 This also suggests that 2p47, a proposition traditionally considered vexing, may be much less cryptic than it appears; for discussion, see Viljanen 2014a.

25 This is the example Spinoza gives in TIE, §96.

26 TIE, §72 reads: "E.g., to form the concept of a sphere, I feign a cause at will, say that a semicircle is rotated around a center, and that the sphere is, as it were, produced by this rotation. This idea, of course, is true, and even though we may know that no sphere in nature was ever produced in this way, nevertheless, this perception is true, and a very easy way of forming the concept of a sphere."

27 Again, for more on these issues, see Viljanen 2020. See also chapter 3.

28 See section 6.5.

29 See section 3.2.

30 For discussion, see Della Rocca 2003.

31 In Epp. 81 and 83, Spinoza explicitly criticizes the Cartesian notion of extension as intrinsically inert; for discussion, see Viljanen 2007.

32 See 2p49s (G II, 131); but also Viljanen 2014a.

33 D. Steinberg 2005: 149–52.

34 The example is traditional, borrowed from Descartes and Aristotle.

35 The scholium continues: "For if the same mind, while it imagined nonexistent things as present to it, at the same time knew that those things did not exist, it would, of course, attribute this power of imagining to a virtue of its nature – not to a vice[.]"

36 For more on this, see J. Steinberg 2018b.

37 This idea is crucial for Spinoza's moral philosophy; see sections 6.3–4.

38 Gilbert 1991: 107.

39 Gilbert 1991; Gilbert, Tafarodi, and Malone 1993.

40 In chapter 7, we will explore this in detail.

Chapter 5 Action and Emotion

1 Recall section 3.1.

2 As we will see, this is a debated issue, the main question of which is, as Steven Nadler (2006: 198) puts it, "whether or not Spinoza, contrary to

what would seem to be the lesson of the *Ethics* so far, is surreptitiously and (it has been argued) illegitimately introducing teleology into nature."

3 The first three sections of this chapter have been adapted from Viljanen 2015.

4 See, e.g., Della Rocca 1996; Garrett 2002; Lin 2004; Viljanen 2011: ch. 4.

5 It should be noted that the concept of power has never been considered similarly problematic in the French tradition, as such classic readings as Deleuze (1992) and Matheron (1969) evince.

6 See section 2.4.

7 Cohen 1964.

8 This is, more or less, the mainstream view; for discussion, see, e.g., Garrett 2009; Viljanen 2014b. See also section 6.5 below.

9 See Viljanen 2011: ch. 6; J. Steinberg 2018a: ch. 1.

10 For an account of the basic emotions, see section 5.4.

11 See section 5.4.

12 See also 3p39s.

13 Recall sections 3.1–2.

14 This is merely a rough approximation; for a much more fine-grained analysis of the desire-relativity of moral judgments, see sections 5.4 and 6.1–2.

15 In section 6.2, our account of Spinoza's axiology shows the way in which it is based on the notion of power of *acting*.

16 For more on this, see esp. Viljanen 2011: ch. 1, but also Hübner 2015.

17 See Epp. 43 and 75.

18 McDonough 2011: 180.

19 For discussion, see Carriero 2005: 146–7; Viljanen 2011: ch. 6; J. Steinberg 2011.

20 See, e.g., Bennett 1984, 1990; Carriero 2005; Garrett 1999; Lin 2006; J. Steinberg 2011; Viljanen 2010, 2011: ch. 5.

21 Spinoza sometimes emphasizes the bodily dimension to affects, identifying them with "constitutions of the body" (3p18d), while at other points he emphasizes the mental side, as when he links affect with "passion of the mind" (defaff3exp).

22 Cf. 3p18d.

23 See section 4.2.

24 Elisabeth presents her request in the September 13, 1645 letter to Descartes.

25 See esp. *Passions* II.138 (CSM I, 376–7); but also I.48 and I.28 (CSM I, 347 and 339).

26 For a version of this in Stoicism, see Long and Sedley 1987, I, 65K.

27 Descartes allows that even if the "proximate cause" of passion is a disturbance of the pineal gland, objects of perception are typically the "first" or "principal" cause (see *Passions* II.51; CSM I, 349).

28 For a detailed discussion of this, see section 6.1. For a further defense, see J. Steinberg 2016.

29 It is worth noting that in the early *Short Treatise*, the passions that are first discussed are wonder, love, hate, and desire (KV II.3; G I, 56–8).

30 See defaff6–7.

31 See *Passions* II.70; CSM I, 353. See also 3p52s.

32 See also TTP 6.

33 For a thorough discussion of this point, see LeBuffe 2010: 203–10.

34 See James 1997.

35 See Frijda 1999. For a full discussion, see J. Steinberg 2016.

36 See also 4p15, 4p15d, 4p60.

37 Viljanen 2011: 137–8.

38 This point is worked out in greater detail in J. Steinberg 2016 and 2018a: ch. 1.

39 See gendefaff; G II, 203.

40 Recall the discussion of the nature of inadequate knowledge in section 4.3.

41 We will discuss this in detail in section 6.3.

42 For more on this, see section 6.4.

43 Again, see section 6.4.

44 J. Steinberg 2013.

45 See Ferrari and Gallese 2007; Simner 1971.

46 See also defaff34, 3p24s.

Chapter 6 Moral Philosophy

1 Recall chapter 3.

2 See section 3.2.

3 See, e.g., Ep. 32.

4 As Spinoza famously puts it in the so-called "Physical Digression" between 2p13 and 2p14: "When a number of bodies, whether of the same or of different size, are so constrained by other bodies that they lie upon one another, or if they so move, whether with the same degree or different degrees of speed, *that they communicate their motions to each other in a certain fixed manner*, we shall say that those bodies are united with one another and that they all together compose one body *or* individual, which is distinguished from the others by this union of bodies" (2p13le3def, the first emphasis added).

5 Dropsy, a condition similar to what we would call edema today, was invoked in idealized form by early modern philosophers to indicate a condition in which further hydration is actually injurious to one's health.

6 Recall section 1.2.

7 See section 4.3.

8 It is worth noting that Spinoza does not oppose all pursuits of sensual pleasure, which can be restorative when pursued in moderation (4p45s).

9 Recall section 5.5.

10 See section 5.4.

11 This explains the difficulty that many young children experienced in Walter Mischel's (1968) famous marshmallow experiment. In the experiment, the children were given one marshmallow while being promised a second one if they could resist eating the first while the experimenter was out of the room. The hot stimulus of the present marshmallow is more powerful than the cool, less intense representation of two marshmallows in the temporally distant future.

12 This is the position that is famously defended by Hume (*Enquiry* 8.2).

13 See section 5.2.

14 Again, recall section 5.2.

15 For discussion, see Curley 1988: 104–8, 119–26.

16 Curley (1973), for instance, characterizes the dictates of reason as hypothetical imperatives with a necessarily instantiated antecedent, which means that they are rules for successful empowerment, which is something that we all necessarily want.

17 Rutherford 2008.

18 See 4p59s.

19 This fits with his division of rational affects (related to strength of character) into tenacity and nobility; see section 5.5.

20 For more on this, see Hübner 2016; Viljanen 2018.

21 See J. Steinberg 2019.

22 Garrett 1990a; see also Youpa 2009.

23 For more on this, see J. Steinberg 2014.

24 Bennett 1984: 336.

25 As Spinoza explains, envy is "hate, insofar as it is considered so to dispose a man that he is glad at another's ill fortune and saddened by his good fortune" (3p24s).

26 See, e.g., Bennett 1984: ch. 4; Lin 2009.

27 For the most damning words, see Bennett 1984: 372–5. For more sympathetic discussions, see, e.g., Curley 1988: 83–6; Garrett 2009.

28 The first half of this section is adapted from J. Steinberg 2018a: ch. 8.

29 See section 5.1.

30 See also 1p24c.

31 For more on this, see Viljanen 2011: ch. 6.

32 For a thorough analysis that persuasively defends this position, see Nadler 2001: ch. 5.

33 Recall that love is, according to Spinoza, "joy with the accompanying idea of an external cause" (3p13s).

34 Here we are talking specifically about intellectual love of God; for a potential difference between it and lower forms of loving God, as well as for an account concerning the context for Spinoza's view, see Nadler 2018.

Chapter 7 Political Philosophy

1 Parts of this chapter draw on J. Steinberg 2018a.
2 See section 3.4.
3 Nadler 1999: 305.
4 Freudenthal 1899: 201.
5 Feuer 1958: ch. 5.
6 Most of the De la Courts' writings were published by Pieter de la Court after the death of his brother Johan in 1660. However, because it remains unclear how much Pieter added and how much he profited off his studious younger brother, we will refer to these authors of these writings simply as the De la Courts.
7 Haitsma Mulier 1980; Petry 1984.
8 Cf. Machiavelli's *Prince* I.15.
9 Recall chapters 2–3.
10 Cf. TP 2/8, 2/4.
11 Cf. TP 2/12.
12 See Negri 1991; J. Steinberg 2008.
13 Cf. TTP 17.5–6; G III, 201–2.
14 See section 6.2.
15 See J. Steinberg 2018a: ch. 4.
16 See, e.g., TP 5/6.
17 See TP 1/1.
18 See section 6.4.
19 See section 6.2.
20 See section 3.5.
21 See TTP 20.17; G III, 242.
22 Cf. TTP 14.20; G III, 176.
23 Curley 1996; Feuer 1958.
24 Balibar 1989: 128. Regrettably and notoriously, Spinoza excludes women – along with foreigners and servants – from citizenship.
25 Cf. TTP 20.37–8; G III, 245.
26 Cf. TP 6/8.
27 See, e.g., TP 8/44, 9/14.

Chapter 8 Spinoza's Reception

1 The ensuing exposition draws heavily on Beiser 1987; Israel 2001; and Moreau and Lærke (forthcoming); and to lesser extent on Newlands 2011; Forster 2012; van Bunge 2012.
2 It took nearly a century until there appeared a work deemed anywhere near as blasphemous as Spinoza's *oeuvre*, namely Baron d'Holbach's *Système de la nature, ou Des loix du monde physique et du monde moral* (1770).

3 See esp. Israel 2001, but also 2010.

4 Pierre-Daniel Huet's *Demonstratio evangelica* (1679) was perhaps foremost among the clerical responses.

5 See sections 3.5–6.

6 For a classic study of Spinoza's reception in France, see Vernière 1954.

7 Respectively, the German Idealist J. G. Fichte (1762–1814) came to be considered, in the 1790s, the most notable philosopher "of the subject."

8 Of these works, only the one by Deleuze has been translated into English; see Deleuze 1992.

9 The first edition of the work appeared in 1999, the second in 2018.

10 In Germany, a new critical edition of Spinoza's works has appeared during this millennium under the editorship of Wolfgang Bartuschat.

References

Alanen, Lilli. 2003. *Descartes's Concept of Mind.* Cambridge, MA: Harvard University Press.

Aquinas, Thomas. 1955–7. *Summa contra Gentiles* I–IV. Garden City, NY: Image Books.

Aquinas, Thomas. 1981. *Summa Theologiae*, trans. the English Dominicans. New York: Christian Classics.

Aubrey, John. 1898. *Brief Lives* I–II, ed. Andrew Clark. Oxford: Clarendon Press.

Balibar, Étienne. 1989. "Spinoza: The Anti-Orwell: The Fear of the Masses." *Rethinking Marxism: A Journal of Economics, Culture, and Society* 2(3): 104–39.

Beiser, Frederick C. 1987. *The Fate of Reason: German Philosophy from Kant to Fichte.* Cambridge, MA: Harvard University Press.

Bennett, Jonathan. 1984. *A Study of Spinoza's Ethics.* Cambridge: Cambridge University Press.

Bennett, Jonathan. 1990. "Spinoza and Teleology: A Reply to Curley," in Edwin Curley and Pierre-François Moreau (eds), *Spinoza: Issues and Directions: The Proceedings of the Chicago Spinoza Conference*, pp. 53–7. Leiden: Brill.

Broughton, Janet. 2002. *Descartes's Method of Doubt.* Princeton: Princeton University Press.

Brown, Deborah J. 2006. *Descartes and the Passionate Mind.* Cambridge: Cambridge University Press.

Carriero, John. 1995. "On the Relationship between Mode and Substance in Spinoza's Metaphysics." *Journal of the History of Philosophy* 33(2): 245–73.

Carriero, John. 2005. "Spinoza on Final Causality," in Daniel Garber and Steven Nadler (eds), *Oxford Studies in Early Modern Philosophy*, Vol. II, pp. 105–47. Oxford: Clarendon Press.

Carriero. John. 2009. *Between Two Worlds: A Reading of Descartes's Meditations*. Princeton: Princeton University Press.

Cohen, I. Bernard. 1964. "'Quantum in se est': Newton's Concept of Inertia in Relation to Descartes and Lucretius." *Notes and Records of the Royal Society of London* 19(2): 131–55.

Cottingham, John. 1986. *Descartes*. Oxford: Blackwell.

Curley, Edwin. 1969. *Spinoza's Metaphysics: An Essay in Interpretation*. Cambridge, MA: Harvard University Press.

Curley, Edwin. 1973. "Spinoza's Moral Philosophy," in Marjorie Grene (ed.), *Spinoza: A Collection of Critical Essays*, pp. 354–76. Garden City, NY: Anchor.

Curley, Edwin. 1985. "General Preface," in Edwin Curley (ed. and trans.), *The Collected Works of Spinoza*, pp. ix–xvii. Princeton: Princeton University Press.

Curley, Edwin. 1988. *Behind the Geometrical Method: A Reading of Spinoza's Ethics*. Princeton: Princeton University Press.

Curley, Edwin. 1996. "Kissinger, Spinoza, and Genghis Khan," in Don Garrett (ed.), *Cambridge Companion to Spinoza*, pp. 315–42. Cambridge: Cambridge University Press.

Curley, Edwin and Walski, Gregory. 1999. "Spinoza's Necessitarianism Reconsidered," in Rocco J. Gennaro and Charles Huenemann (eds), *New Essays on the Rationalists*, pp. 241–62. New York: Oxford University Press.

Deleuze, Gilles. 1992. *Expressionism in Philosophy: Spinoza*, trans. Martin Joughin. New York: Zone Books.

Della Rocca, Michael. 1996. *Representation and the Mind–Body Problem in Spinoza*. New York: Oxford University Press.

Della Rocca, Michael. 2002. "Spinoza's Substance Monism," in Olli Koistinen and John Biro (eds), *Spinoza: Metaphysical Themes*, pp. 11–37. New York: Oxford University Press.

Della Rocca, Michael. 2003. "The Power of an Idea: Spinoza's Critique of Pure Will." *Noûs* 37(2): 200–31.

Della Rocca, Michael. 2008. *Spinoza*. London: Routledge.

Ferrari, Vittorio and Gallese, Pier Francesco. 2007. "Mirror Neurons and Intersubjectivity," in Stein Bråten (ed.), *On Being Moved: From Mirror Neurons to Empathy*, pp. 73–88. Amsterdam: John Benjamins.

Feuer, Lewis. 1958. *Spinoza and the Rise of Liberalism*. Boston, MA: Beacon Press.

Forster, Michael N. 2012. "Herder and Spinoza," in Eckart Förster and Yitzhak Y. Melamed (eds), *Spinoza and German Idealism*, pp. 59–84. Cambridge: Cambridge University Press.

Freudenthal, Jakob. 1899. *Die Lebensgeschichte Spinoza's in Quellenschriften, Urkunden and Nichtamtlichen Nachrichten*. Leipzig: Verlag Von Veit.

Frijda, Nico. 1999. "Spinoza and Current Theory of Emotion," in Yirmiyahu Yovel (ed.), *Desire and Affect: Spinoza as Psychologist*, pp. 235–61. New York: Little Room Press.

Garber, Daniel. 2001. *Descartes Embodied: Reading Cartesian Philosophy through Cartesian Science*. Cambridge: Cambridge University Press.

Garrett, Don. 1979. "Spinoza's 'Ontological' Argument." *The Philosophical Review* 88(2): 198–223.

Garrett, Don. 1990a. "'A Free Man Always Acts Honestly, Not Deceptively': Freedom and the Good in Spinoza's *Ethics*," in Edwin Curley and Pierre-François Moreau (eds), *Spinoza: Issues and Directions*, pp. 221–38. Leiden: Brill.

Garrett, Don. 1990b. "*Ethics* IP5: Shared Attributes and the Basis of Spinoza's Monism," in J. A. Cover and Mark Kulstad (eds), *Central Themes in Early Modern Philosophy: Essays Presented to Jonathan Bennett*, pp. 69–107. Indianapolis: Hackett.

Garrett, Don. 1991. "Spinoza's Necessitarianism," in Yirmiyahu Yovel (ed.), *God and Nature: Spinoza's Metaphysics*, pp. 191–218. Leiden: Brill.

Garrett, Don. 1999. "Teleology in Spinoza and Early Modern Rationalism," in Rocco J. Gennaro and Charles Huenemann (eds), *New Essays on the Rationalists*, pp. 310–35. New York: Oxford University Press.

Garrett, Don. 2002. "Spinoza's Conatus Argument," in Olli Koistinen and John Biro (eds), *Spinoza: Metaphysical Themes*, pp. 127–58. Oxford: Oxford University Press.

Garrett, Don. 2009. "Spinoza on the Essence of the Human Body and the Part of the Mind That Is Eternal," in Olli Koistinen (ed.), *The Cambridge Companion to Spinoza's* Ethics, pp. 284–302. Cambridge: Cambridge University Press.

Gilbert, Daniel T. 1991. "How Mental Systems Believe." *American Psychologist* 46(2): 107–19.

Gilbert, Daniel T., Tafarodi, R. W., and Malone, P. S. 1993. "You Can't Not Believe Everything You Read." *Journal of Personality and Social Psychology* 65(2): 221–33.

Gueroult, Martial. 1968. *Spinoza I. Dieu (*Éthique, *I)*. Paris: Aubier-Montaigne.

Gueroult, Martial. 1974. *Spinoza II. L'Âme (*Éthique, *II)*. Paris: Aubier-Montaigne.

Haitsma Mulier, Eco. 1980. *The Myth of Venice and Dutch Republican Thought in the Seventeenth Century*, trans. Gerard T. Moran. Assen: Van Gorcum.

Haldane, John. 1989. "Voluntarism and Realism in Medieval Ethics." *Journal of Medical Ethics* 15(1): 39–44.

Hampshire, Stuart. 1951. *Spinoza*. Harmondsworth: Pelican Books.

Hoffman, Paul. 1986. "The Unity of Descartes's Man." *The Philosophical Review* 95(3): 339–70.

Hübner, Karolina. 2015. "On the Significance of Formal Causes in Spinoza's Metaphysics." *Archiv für Geschichte der Philosophie* 97(1): 196–233.

Hübner, Karolina. 2016. "Spinoza on Essences, Universals, and Beings of Reason." *Pacific Philosophical Quarterly* 97(1): 58–88.

Hume, David. 2007. *An Enquiry Concerning the Human Understanding*, ed. Peter Millican. Oxford: Oxford University Press.

Israel, Jonathan. 1995. *The Dutch Republic: Its Rise, Greatness and Fall, 1477–1806*. Oxford: Clarendon Press.

Israel, Jonathan. 2001. *Radical Enlightenment: Philosophy and the Making of Modernity 1650–1750*. Oxford: Oxford University Press.

Israel, Jonathan. 2010. *A Revolution of the Mind: Radical Enlightenment and the Intellectual Origins of Modern Democracy*. Princeton: Princeton University Press.

James, Susan. 1997. *Passion and Action: The Emotions in Seventeenth-Century Philosophy*. Oxford: Clarendon Press.

Jarrett, Charles. 2009. "Spinoza on Necessity," in Olli Koistinen (ed.), *The Cambridge Companion to Spinoza's Ethics*, pp. 118–39. Cambridge: Cambridge University Press.

Klever, W. N. A. 1996. "Spinoza's Life and Works," in Don Garrett (ed.), *The Cambridge Companion to Spinoza*, pp. 13–60. Cambridge: Cambridge University Press.

LeBuffe, Michael. 2010. *From Bondage to Freedom: Spinoza on Human Excellence*. Oxford: Oxford University Press.

Lin, Martin. 2004. "Spinoza's Metaphysics of Desire: The Demonstration of IIIP6." *Archiv für Geschichte der Philosophie* 86(1): 21–55.

Lin, Martin. 2006. "Teleology and Human Action in Spinoza." *The Philosophical Review* 115(3): 317–54.

Lin, Martin. 2009. "The Power of Reason in Spinoza," in Olli Koistinen (ed.), *The Cambridge Companion to Spinoza's Ethics*, pp. 258–83. Cambridge: Cambridge University Press.

Long, A. A. and Sedley, D. N. 1987. *The Hellenistic Philosophers*, I–II. Cambridge: Cambridge University Press.

Machiavelli, Niccolò. 1988. *The Prince*, trans. Russell Price, ed. Quentin Skinner. Cambridge: Cambridge University Press.

Marshall, Eugene. 2013. *The Spiritual Automaton: Spinoza's Science of the Mind*. Oxford: Oxford University Press.

Matheron, Alexandre. 1969. *Individu et communauté chez Spinoza*. Paris: Les Éditions de Minuit.

McDonough, Jeffrey K. 2011. "The Heyday of Teleology and Early Modern Philosophy." *Midwest Studies in Philosophy* 35(1): 179–204.

Melamed, Yitzhak Y. 2013. *Spinoza's Metaphysics: Substance and Thought*. Oxford: Oxford University Press.

Mischel, Walter. 1968. *Personality and Assessment*. New York: Wiley.

Moreau, Pierre-François and Lærke, Mogens. Forthcoming. "Spinoza's Reception," in Don Garrett (ed.), *The Cambridge Companion to Spinoza* (2nd edn). Cambridge: Cambridge University Press.

Nadler, Steven. 1999. *Spinoza: A Life*. Cambridge: Cambridge University Press.

Nadler, Steven. 2001. *Spinoza's Heresy: Immortality and the Jewish Mind*. Oxford: Clarendon Press.

Nadler, Steven. 2006. *Spinoza's* Ethics: *An Introduction*. Cambridge: Cambridge University Press.

Nadler, Steven. 2008. "Spinoza and Consciousness." *Mind* 117(467): 575–601.

Nadler, Steven. 2018. "The Intellectual Love of God," in Michael Della Rocca (ed.), *The Oxford Handbook of Spinoza*, pp. 295–313. Oxford: Oxford University Press.

Negri, Antonio. 1991. *The Savage Anomaly*, trans. Michael Hardt. Minneapolis, MN: University of Minnesota Press.

Newlands, Samuel. 2011. "More Recent Idealist Readings of Spinoza." *Philosophy Compass* 6(2): 109–19.

Petry, Michael. 1984. "Hobbes and the Early Dutch Spinozists," in Cornelius de Deugd (ed.), *Spinoza's Political and Theological Thought*, pp. 63–72. Amsterdam: North-Holland Publishing.

Russell, Bertrand. 1945. *History of Western Philosophy*. New York: Simon and Schuster.

Rutherford, Donald. 2008. "Spinoza and the Dictates of Reason." *Inquiry* 51(5): 485–511.

Shein, Noa. 2009. "The False Dichotomy between Objective and Subjective Interpretations of Spinoza's Theory of Attributes." *British Journal for the History of Philosophy* 17(3): 505–32.

Simmons, Alison. 2017. "Mind–Body Union and the Limits of Cartesian Metaphysics." *Philosophers' Imprint* 17(14): 1–26.

Simner, Mark L. 1971. "Newborn's Response to the Cry of Another Infant." *Developmental Psychology* 5(1): 136–50.

Steinberg, Diane. 2000. *On Spinoza*. Belmont, CA: Wadsworth.

Steinberg, Diane. 2005. "Belief, Affirmation, and the Doctrine of *Conatus* in Spinoza." *The Southern Journal of Philosophy* 43(1): 147–58.

Steinberg, Justin. 2008. "On Being *Sui Iuris*: Spinoza and the Republican Idea of Liberty." *History of European Ideas* 34(3): 239–49.

Steinberg, Justin. 2011. "Spinoza on Human Purposiveness and Mental Causation." *Logical Analysis and the History of Philosophy* 14(1): 51–70.

Steinberg, Justin. 2013. "Imitation, Representation, and Humanity in Spinoza's *Ethics*." *Journal of the History of Philosophy* 51(3): 383–407.

Steinberg, Justin. 2014. "Following a *Recta Ratio Vivendi*: The Practical Utility of Spinoza's Dictates of Reason," in Matthew J. Kisner and Andrew Youpa (eds), *Essays on Spinoza's Ethical Theory*, pp. 178–96. Oxford: Oxford University Press.

Steinberg, Justin. 2016. "Affect, Desire, and Judgement in Spinoza's Account of Motivation." *British Journal for the History of Philosophy* 24(1): 67–87.

Steinberg, Justin. 2018a. *Spinoza's Political Psychology: The Taming of Fortune and Fear*. Cambridge: Cambridge University Press.

Steinberg, Justin. 2018b. "Two Puzzles Concerning Spinoza's Conception of Belief." *European Journal of Philosophy* 26(1): 261–82.

Steinberg, Justin. 2019. "Bodies Politic and Civic Agreement," in Aurelia

Armstrong, Keith Green, and Andrea Sangiacomo (eds), *Spinoza and Relational Autonomy: Being with Others*, pp. 132–48. Edinburgh: Edinburgh University Press.

Van Bunge, Wiep. 2012. *Spinoza Past and Present: Essays on Spinoza, Spinozism, and Spinoza Scholarship*. Leiden: Brill.

Vernière, Paul. 1954. *Spinoza et la pensée française avant la revolution* I–II. Paris: Presses universitaires de France.

Viljanen, Valtteri. 2007. "Field Metaphysic, Power, and Individuation in Spinoza." *Canadian Journal of Philosophy* 37(3): 393–418.

Viljanen, Valtteri. 2009. "Spinoza's Ontology," in Olli Koistinen (ed.), *The Cambridge Companion to Spinoza's* Ethics, pp. 56–78. Cambridge: Cambridge University Press.

Viljanen, Valtteri. 2010. "Causal Efficacy of Representational Content in Spinoza." *History of Philosophy Quarterly* 27(1): 17–34.

Viljanen, Valtteri. 2011. *Spinoza's Geometry of Power*. Cambridge: Cambridge University Press.

Viljanen, Valtteri. 2014a. "Spinoza on Activity in Sense Perception," in José Filipe Silva and Mikko Yrjönsuuri (eds), *Active Perception in the History of Philosophy: From Plato to Modern Philosophy*, pp. 241–54. Dordrecht: Springer.

Viljanen, Valtteri. 2014b. "Spinoza on Virtue and Eternity," in Matthew J. Kisner and Andrew Youpa (eds), *Essays on Spinoza's Ethical Theory*, pp. 258–71. Oxford: Oxford University Press.

Viljanen, Valtteri. 2015. "Theory of *Conatus*," in André Santos Campos (ed.), *Spinoza: Basic Concepts*, pp. 95–105. Exeter: Imprint Academic.

Viljanen, Valtteri. 2018. "Spinoza's Ontology Geometrically Illustrated: A Reading of *Ethics* IIP8S," in Beth Lord (ed.), *Spinoza's Philosophy of Ratio*, pp. 5–18. Edinburgh: Edinburgh University Press.

Viljanen, Valtteri. 2020. "The Young Spinoza on Scepticism, Truth, and Method." *Canadian Journal of Philosophy* 50(1): 130–42.

Youpa, Andrew. 2009. "Spinoza's Theory of the Good," in Olli Koistinen (ed.), *The Cambridge Companion to Spinoza's* Ethics, pp. 242–57. Cambridge: Cambridge University Press.

Yovel, Yirmiyahu. 1989. *Spinoza and Other Heretics* I–II. Princeton: Princeton University Press.

Index